Monks and Muslims II

MONASTIC INTERRELIGIOUS DIALOGUE SERIES

Monks and Muslims II

Creating Communities of Friendship

Edited by
Mohammad Ali Shomali
and
William Skudlarek

LITURGICAL PRESS
Collegeville, Minnesota

www.litpress.org

Cover design by Ann Blattner.

Excerpts from documents of the Second Vatican Council are from *Vatican Council II: The Basic Sixteen Documents*, by Austin Flannery, OP © 1996 (Costello Publishing Company, Inc.). Used with permission.

Unless otherwise noted, biblical texts in this work are taken from the *New Revised Standard Version Bible*: Catholic Edition © 1989, 1993, Division of Christian Education of the National Council of the Churches of Christ in the United States of America. Used by permission. All rights reserved.

Excerpts from the Rule of Saint Benedict are from *Rule of Saint Benedict 1980*, edited by Timothy Fry (Collegeville, MN: Liturgical Press, 1981) © 1981 by The Order of Saint Benedict, Inc., Collegeville, Minnesota. All rights reserved.

Unless otherwise noted, texts from the Qurʾan are taken from the translation by ʿAli Quli Qaraʾi © 2005 by The Islamic College for Advanced Studies (ICAS). All rights reserved.

Unless otherwise noted, translations from non-English sources are provided by the respective authors in this book.

1   2   3   4   5   6   7   8   9

Library of Congress Cataloging-in-Publication Data

Monks and Muslims II : creating communities of friendship / edited by Mohammad Ali Shomali and William Skudlarek.
    pages cm — (Monastic interreligious dialogue series)
    Includes bibliographical references.
    ISBN 978-0-8146-3811-8 — ISBN 978-0-8146-3836-1 (ebook)
    1. Islam—Relations—Christianity.   2. Christianity and other religions—Islam.   3. Dialogue—Religious aspects—Islam.
4. Dialogue—Religious aspects—Christianity.   I. Shomali, Mohammad A., 1965–   II. Skudlarek, William.
    BP172.M645 2014
    261.2'7—dc23   2013041022

Contents

Introduction

"Monks and Muslims: Creating Communities of Friendship" was the theme of a Monastic/Muslim dialogue that took place in Qum, Iran, from September 28 to October 3, 2012. The fifteen Muslim participants were professors, administrators, researchers, and students from various universities and educational institutes in Qum, especially the International Institute for Islamic Studies, whose Director is Dr. Mohammad Ali Shomali. The nine Benedictine and Cistercian participants came from monastic communities in Belgium, England, France, Germany, Holland, Italy, Kenya, and the United States. The conference was jointly sponsored by the International Institute for Islamic Studies and *Dialogue Interreligieux Monastique*·Monastic Interreligious Dialogue.

The conference theme was divided into four subsections: The Place of Friendship in the Bible and the Qur'an, Friendship as a Spiritual Discipline for Monks and Muslims, Friendship as the Prerequisite and Goal of Monastic/Muslim Dialogue, and From Enmity to Amity: Remembering the Past, Envisioning the Future. These published proceedings do not present the papers in the order they were given but rather begin with two chapters that deal with concrete instances of Christian/Muslim relations, one from the recent past (Christian de Chergé and the Cistercian community of Tibhirine in Algeria) and the other from the first century of Islam (the Prophet Muhammad and his first followers). The chapters that follow then explore the scriptural, theological, spiritual, philosophical, and practical bases for friendship between monks and Muslims.

Most of us who came together in Qum had taken part in a Monastic/Muslim dialogue in Rome the previous year.[1] The follow-up meeting in Qum was therefore an occasion to deepen the bonds of friendship that had already been established. The monastic participants were deeply moved by the warm, generous, and always attentive hospitality not only of the Iranians who hosted the conference but also of the Iranian people at large, many of whom were intrigued by our monastic garb—which we also wore when going from our hotel to the conference site and when visiting shrines and educational institutions—and would approach us to ask who we were and to welcome us to their country.

Qum is the most important religious and educational center in Iran, and its numerous shrines and schools give evidence of how much ritual prayer (*salāt*), supplication (*du'a*), pilgrimage, and theological/philosophical reflection shape the Shi'a tradition of Islam. There are some 60,000 seminarians in Qum, in addition to thousands of other students, many of them women, who are enrolled in the various institutions of higher learning in the city. In the area of religion, most study and research is understandably focused on Islam, but Qum also has a University of Religions and Denominations, which we visited, and Dr. Shomali's Institute has as one of its goals the training of professional and competent researchers to introduce Islam in general and Shi'ite Islam in particular in religious and scientific centers in the country or abroad and in international seminars and interfaith dialogues.

[1] The papers given at that meeting have been published: *Monks and Muslims: Monastic and Shi'a Spirituality in Dialogue* (Collegeville, MN: Liturgical Press, 2012). The meeting in Rome followed upon three meetings between Catholics and Iranian Shi'a Muslims that had taken place in England. The proceedings of those three conferences were recently reissued by Melisende Publishing in London: *Catholics and Shi'a in Dialogue: Studies in Theology and Spirituality* (2004); *A Catholic Shi'a Engagement: Faith and Reason in Theory and Practice* (2006); *A Catholic-Shi'a Dialogue: Ethics in Today's Society* (2008).

Ritual and personal prayer gave a particularly monastic tone to this dialogue. Visits to various mosques and shrines provided opportunities for personal prayer and meditation. Monastic Lauds and Vespers were prayed before and after the formal sessions of the dialogue, but the monastic hour of Sext (midday prayer) and the Muslim *dhuhr* (noon prayer) took place in the prayer room of the International Institute for Islamic Studies, with monks and Muslims silently participating in each other's ritual prayer.

May continued prayer and dialogue extend the bonds of friendship to an ever larger number of Christians and Muslims, so that in God's good time friendship may become the most common and fitting way to describe the relationship between the followers of these two religions.

William Skudlarek

Friendship in Tibhirine

Monastic/Muslim Dialogue in Algeria

Godefroy Raguenet de Saint-Albin

"Friendship is something mysterious. Something big. . . . It is broad. It is deep. It is beautiful. It is good. It is true."[1] These words of Brother Christophe, poet and monk of Tibhirine, introduce us to the different dimensions of the mystery of friendship. Speaking of friendship as a mystery does not mean declaring it to be the exclusive privilege of believers, be they Muslim or Christian. But it certainly acknowledges the ability of believers to recognize friendship as a gift of God. Our focus here leads us one step further, since we will be using the example of the community of Tibhirine to speak of a friendship that can unite Muslims and Christian monks on their way to God.[2]

Tibhirine shows us that when we speak of friendship, we need to speak concretely. Friendship calls for experiential truth, beyond just good ideas. It is an experience that is fully human, and therefore can be truly spiritual, that is, related to the always

[1] Christophe Lebreton, *Aime jusqu'au bout du feu* [Poems of Brother Christophe] (Paris: Editions Monte Cristo, 1997), p. 108. Most of the writings of the monks of Tibhirine have not yet been translated into English.

[2] A personal note: Although I never met the martyred monks of Tibhirine, the testimony of their life and death is, in large part, what led me to monastic life. Their writings introduced me to their experience. I also shared daily life with the two survivors of the Tibhirine community during several stays at the Trappist monastery in Morocco over the past four years.

greater mystery of God, *Allahu akbar!*, to God who is greater than us and all our thoughts, feelings, and deeds, while being mysteriously present and provident to all of his creation and merciful to all human beings.

Tibhirine was a community of Cistercian monks who for years remained totally hidden in the Muslim region of the Maghreb. It was fragile, composed of brothers who, humanly speaking, had little in common. Because of their dramatic kidnapping and execution, the light of martyrdom, *shahadâ*, shone on them and testified to their love for God and the people of Algeria. Theirs is a very real story, fashioned by humanity, earth, hospitality, religion—a story for which the experience of friendship was foundational. It is also a story that needs to be placed in the broader history of the place where this monastic presence was planted and then grew until it was uprooted during a decade of violence.

Some Benchmarks in the Story of Monasticism in Algeria

To situate the story of the monastic community of Tibhirine in the long and rich history of Algeria, one would have to reach back to the centuries in which Christianity flourished in North Africa, to the figure of Saint Augustine, to the country's divisions, to the Muslim conquest.[3] If we limit ourselves to the more recent history of a monastic presence in Algeria, we see that Trappist monks arrived only thirteen years after the French conquest in 1830. One figure from this period who should be mentioned is Sheikh Abd-el-Kader, chief of the local resistance and a prominent politician, but also a Sufi of great stature. He was a close friend of the first bishop of Alger, Antoine-Louis-Adolphe Dupuch. After his exile in France, Sheikh Abd-el-Kader was responsible for saving many Christian lives in Syria.

---

[3] During his time at the Pontifical Institute for Arabic and Islamic Studies in Rome, De Chergé, future superior of the Tibhirine community, studied the spiritual history of Algeria.

The first monastic settlement was established in Staouëli, seventeen kilometers north of Alger, in 1843.[4] It rapidly acquired a certain notoriety thanks to the rapid economic development made possible by the use of modern agricultural techniques. This was precisely the reason it was supported by the French political authorities, even though they were mostly antireligious. Right from the beginning, therefore, the monastery was saddled with all the ambiguities of a colonial system. In line with the thinking of the time, it was founded to bring "civilization" to a barbaric population. Even so, Sheikh Abd-el-Kader valued the religious presence of the monks and explicitly praised Dom François-Regis, the first abbot, for their sense of hospitality.[5] Nonetheless, the monastery had to close in 1904 because of antireligious laws.

Thirty years later, a second monastery was established in the area of Médéa, at Tibhirine (the name means "the garden").[6] This time its style and spirit were different; its search for ways to collaborate with the local population brought it much closer to the sense of brotherhood exemplified by the former Trappist Charles de Foucauld.[7] Thanks to its acceptance (one could even

---

[4] The founding monastery was Notre-Dame d'Aiguebelle, in southeastern France, at the time a large community of about two hundred monks.

[5] "I have heard about you a long time ago because my men spoke of you monks. You always received them as though they were your own brothers." In John W. Kiser, *The Monks of Tibhirine* (New York: St. Martin's Press, 2002), p. 37.

[6] The community of Our Lady of Atlas began as a refuge for a group of monks in exile from Slovenia who came to Ouled-Trift (Algeria) in 1934. The community was transferred to Ben Chicao in 1935 and then to Tibhirine, seven kilometers from Médéa, in 1938. It was later assumed by the French abbey of Aiguebelle, which sent some monks to the community. Soon thereafter the foundation became an autonomous monastic community.

[7] Charles de Foucauld, emblematic Christian figure of the time, "converted back" to the Christianity of his childhood through his encounter with Islam in Morocco. He became a Trappist monk in France and Syria and then left the Trappists to start an amazing spiritual journey toward universal brotherhood in Palestine, Morocco, and Algeria among Touareg

say "adoption") by its neighbors, the community managed to pass through the war of independence (1954–1962) unscathed. But the situation of the Algerian Church had by then changed dramatically. Most of its members, the one million of *"pied-noirs"* (Frenchmen born in Algeria), departed for France in a massive exodus, leaving behind only a tiny remnant of Catholics. The energy of Archbishop Léon-Etienne Duval of Alger, who had clearly supported the Algerian population and its legitimate desire for independence, convinced the monks to stay, despite the impossibility of local recruitment (conversion was not allowed). He believed the mere presence of a Christian monastic community, whatever the nationality of its members, in the midst of a Muslim people, was of capital importance.

Following independence, successive governments maintained a mixture of authoritarian socialism and Muslim law, but were marred by a high level of corruption. In 1990 the Islamist party won a large majority of votes in the first free elections. In elections for the legislature in 1992, the Islamist party had similar success in the first round, but the army cancelled the second round of voting. Violence then erupted between the ruling powers and factions of the GIA (*Groupe Islamiste Armé* [Armed Islamist Group]). Two years later the murders of foreigners and Christians began.

The community, whose life was devoted to work and prayer, became more and more committed to daily dialogue with its Muslim hosts and so decided to stay in spite of the danger. On December 24, 1993, Christmas Eve, the monastery was "visited" by the same Armed Islamist Group that had killed twelve Croatian Christian workers, friends of the monastery. The Prior, Christian de Chergé, resisted the demands of the leader, Saya Attya. For a while the community seems to have benefited from

---

tribes. He was killed in Algeria in 1916. Despite his desire, he never managed to found a community of disciples to continue to live his deep immersion in a Muslim environment. The fruits would come one generation later with the flourishing of communities inspired by his life. We know that each of the seven martyred monks of Tibhirine felt a spiritual bond with Charles de Foucauld.

his "*aman*," until he was killed. On several occasions the monks renewed their decision to stay, choosing to remain faithful to their neighbors and to the God who had called them to search and serve him there. Finally, on the night of March 26–27, 1996, seven monks were captured (two were not found and left behind) and, after being held for two months, were executed, as announced by a communiqué of the GIA dated May 21.[8]

Friendship: A Foundational Experience

Each member of the 1996 Tibhirine community had his own history with Algeria, most of them because they had been, in different ways, involved in the war of 1954–1962. The elder, Brother Luc, a doctor who never ceased to provide medical assistance to the local population, arrived in 1946. Among those who had recently come from other monasteries to join Tibhirine, some had worked with Algerian immigrants in France and often became friends with them. It would be worthwhile to speak for a moment of these various experiences of friendship. I will mainly speak of one: the story of the friendship of Christian de Chergé and Mohammad.[9] I do so not because their friendship was exceptional—although it was, in a sense—but because De Chergé became the superior in charge of the little community of Tibhirine, and his friendship with Mohammad became a gift that he shared with others as he fostered the community's trustful daily dialogue and strove to establish a common horizon of hope.

This story of his friendship with Mohammad, which dated back to 1959, was one that De Chergé related much later on several occasions.

---

[8] It is still uncertain whether or not the police and Algerian secret services were involved in one way or another in this operation. The severed heads of the monks were discovered two days later.

[9] Their names are powerfully symbolic, but they are, in fact, their real names. For the sake of clarity, I will for the most part refer to Father Christian as De Chergé rather than Christian.

Having reached the age of adulthood and confronted—along with the rest of my generation—by the harsh reality of the war [i.e., the War of Independence against France], I was graced to encounter a mature and deeply religious man who set my faith free. He taught me how to live my faith by responding to the tough demands of daily life with simplicity, openness, and surrender to God. Our dialogue was one of peaceful and trusting friendship, whose horizon was the will of God, beyond the turmoil.[10]

Let me simply call attention to some of the features of this relationship between a young seminarian who had been sent to Algeria as an officer and an older Algerian Muslim that made them true friends, in spite of the fact that they were caught in the middle of a war. First, a recognition of the faith, the religion (*iman* and *islam*), and the spiritual value of the other that went beyond deep respect; and secondly, the reciprocity of this relationship, despite its obvious asymmetry. In some ways, it looks like a relationship of spiritual initiation, even though De Chergé was an officer in charge of pacifying the area. At the same time, Mohammad had certainly discerned the precocious spiritual awareness of his young partner in dialogue.

During a common patrol, they were ambushed, and Mohammad intervened, trying to protect De Chergé from the *fellagha*'s fire. The next day he was found murdered next to his well. As De Chergé said later, Mohammad did not want to choose between his brothers and his friend. He would never forget Mohammad's gift of life to save him, and this event became decisive for his call to monastic life. "In the blood of this friend, I understood that my call to follow Christ should sooner or later be lived in the same country where I had received the proof of the greatest love."[11]

All of De Chergé's monastic life will be related to this "pact of blood." More than a debt, this pact developed during the

[10] Christian de Chergé, "Prier en Eglise à l'écoute de l'Islam" in *Chemins de dialogue*, 27 (2006): p. 18.

[11] Ibid.

following years into a vocation: a call to return to Algeria to live a presence of prayer. In fact, knowing that Mohammad's life was at risk because of his cooperation with the French authorities, De Chergé had once promised to pray for him. His friend appreciated his offer but replied, "You will pray for me! But Christians don't know how to pray." To which De Chergé could only confess that prayer was often neglected by Christians and lacked a communitarian visibility. For him, a fraternal Christian presence in Algeria after the drama of war would have to assume a communitarian dimension—which was the unfulfilled wish of Charles de Foucauld. In the aftermath of Independence, when most Christians left the country and the Church was reduced to a tiny group, the community of Tibhirine understood the meaning of its presence in Algeria to be "men of prayer in the midst of men of prayer," thus echoing De Chergé's own wish.

The Sign of the Greatest Love:
Promise and Gage of a Common Future

De Chergé's reference to Mohammad's gift of "the greatest love" recalls Jesus' words to his disciples at his Last Supper with them: "This is my commandment, that you love one another as I have loved you. No one has greater love than this, to lay down one's life for one's friends. You are my friends if you do what I command you" (John 15:12-14). This "greater love" is the love of Jesus, his life offered to his friends-disciples, and sign of the love of God for the whole of humanity, stronger than its fears and violence, stronger than death. But the commandment entrusted by Jesus to his disciples opens up a path of selfless love for everyone, a path that also leads to friendship with him and with the one and only God he calls his Father. It inaugurates the possibility of participation in the divine love that has no boundaries of time, location, or (as De Chergé would add) *religion*. His friend Mohammad, who fulfilled the commandment of love, is the proof and the sign that this promise is for all, and can be received through friendship among believers. This "recognition" in no way annexes Mohammad to Christianity. On the contrary, in God it eludes all barriers of religion. Mohammad's gift of life was in fidelity to his Islam, just like the gift of life made by Jesus, whom De Chergé later liked to contemplate as truly *Muslim*, the servant of God (ʿAbd Allah) whose loving submission (*Islam*) is perfectly fulfilled by the dwelling of His Holy Spirit.[12] His deepest conviction of faith was that his friend already enjoyed the joy of God, with all saints (ʿAwlyy Allah) living in communion with Him.

Furthermore, this event naturally became a "memorial" in De Chergé's religious life. For Christians, the Eucharist is the foundational memorial, the life-giving *dhikr*, of the selfless gift of Jesus. Celebrated every day by the monastic community, this liturgical prayer became for De Chergé a rendezvous with his friend, and it enlivened his hope of a promised communion between Christians and Muslims. Mohammad had become part of this "horizon of the will of God" that he used to share with him.

Thanks to his Muslim friend, De Chergé had taken a giant step on his spiritual journey. For him, this event of the past shed the light of divine promise upon all present relationships between Muslims and Christians. De Chergé became the prophetic watchman, seeking to open, in the midst of a harsh present, the path toward an already foreseen future of communion. Because of the gift he had received, he was now entrusted with the mission of becoming, with his brothers, a living sign of this promise in the land of Algeria.

Hospitality and the "Vulnerability" for Friendship

De Chergé owed his vocation to become a Christian monk in Algeria to a Muslim friend, and his monastic life grew in friendly

---

[12] See Christian de Chergé, "Chrétiens et musulmans. Nos différences ont-elles le sens d'une communion," in *L'Invincible espérance*, Bayard Editions/Centurion (1997), 130–31.

dialogue with Islam. The mystery of Islam fascinated and questioned him, allowing his Christian faith to grow. For him, being a monk in Algeria implied taking the promise-filled risk of a daily encounter with Islam: "Algeria and Islam, it is a Body and a Soul," he would write in his Testament. But it would take time and patience before he could see the realization of his hope, because the community he entered in 1971 did not immediately share his prophetic stance. Many were afraid of his audacious proposals, his commitment to study Arabic and read the Qur'an, to fast during the month of Ramadan—all of which troubled a well-established monastic routine. Despite a long history of daily contact, real generosity, and even a certain friendship with their neighbors, some monks had very little interest in Islam. This was the case with Brother Luc, the *toubib* (doctor), who treated people (bodies and souls) for free, with an incredible dedication and attention to each, doing so from 1946 until the end. He was, far and away, the monk who was most cherished by a grateful population. For De Chergé, Islam was the friend of each day, to whom neighbors and coworkers gave a face as Mohammad did, even if their Islam could be distorted (in particular, as we will see, when Islamism led to barbaric violence and terror).

De Chergé's push for greater dialogue had a decisive impact on the community. Nevertheless, a form of dialogue awakened by hospitality was already constitutive of the life in Tibhirine. Over the years the community came to a deeper understanding of this hospitality, recognizing that it had the specific gift of being a small, poor, and isolated community. The monks began to value their situation of being guests of a foreign country who lived according to a different religious tradition, in which God the All-Merciful is obeyed, served, and loved. Precariousness, relative poverty, and dependence on the good will of their hosts [13] made them vulnerable in two senses: they were more receptive to difference, and thereby open and "vulnerable" to

[13] In 1975 they received an order from the police to leave Algeria within fifteen days. They prepared to do so, but the Archbishop clarified the situation: the order was linked to inner rivalries for political power.

establish friendship with their hosts. To these "searchers of God"[14] on pilgrimage to the Wholly-Other (*Al-Ghayb*), the other (Muslim, Algerian) appeared as a companion, even an ally, since he was himself searching for obedience to God. De Chergé therefore speaks about difference as a "sacrament" of God, a gift that calls for sharing in dialogue and friendship, in order to enrich both and build communion.

It is also no accident that De Chergé was attached to the figure of Abraham, who in both our traditions is an example of sacred hospitality and is uniquely referred to in the Bible's Old Testament as the "friend of God," *Al-Khalîl Allah* (e.g., Isaiah 41:8: "But you, Israel, my servant, Jacob, whom I have chosen, the offspring of Abraham, my friend"). Hospitality is probably one of the best words for friendship, because both experiences have so much in common. Is it not true that to be a friend means being hospitable by opening one's heart to someone else? Is it not to know and hope for one's friend, beyond what the friend knows and hopes for him- or herself, and thereby to open an unexpected future for our friend? De Chergé spoke of spiritual life as a process of (re)birth, in which the friend, the other, the one who is different, is the necessary midwife. But only God is able to move the depths of the human soul, the level at which real friendship comes into being.

As guestmaster—that is, the monk responsible for hospitality in the name of the community—De Chergé was attentive not to offend the faith of Muslim guests by the use of Christian symbols, a kind of courtesy typical of his character and convictions. At one point the community willingly agreed to lend to their neighbors an unoccupied room on the border of the monastery to be used as a mosque. Muezzin and bells in close dialogue! As friendship requires, hospitality had started to become reciprocal. A no less significant sign of this reciprocity was the cooperative work the community developed with several neighbors. After

[14] "Seeking God" is the main indication of a monastic vocation for Saint Benedict, author of our Rule of life.

Independence the monks got rid of most of their land, keeping only what was necessary to provide for their needs. Later on, they decided to work the land together with their neighbors, allocating parcels and sharing machinery, seeds, and water. They also shared the profit of the products (fruits and vegetables) sold on the market. This activity brought the monks into daily and close contact with the population, sharing the hopes, joys and sorrows of the families.

The "Friend of One Night" and Friendship's Openness to the Universal

Soon after his arrival at Tibhirine, De Chergé received confirmation from a Muslim that his hope for common prayer was not in vain. He later recalled this person as "the friend of one night." Following the last community prayer and after he had attended to the needs of the guests, De Chergé liked to remain in the chapel for private prayer. One night in September 1975, the voice of a young Muslim guest began to echo his own prayer to God through Christ. For several hours the chapel resounded with the polyphonic praise of two voices, a marriage of Muslim and Christian prayer, offered in one same Spirit, to the one and only God. Some years later, along with some members of the community, he participated in the *Ribât-es-Salâm*. Created in 1979, it was a group of Christians who were committed to the encounter with Islam. Soon thereafter, it was joined by a group of Sufis of the *tariqa ʿAlawyya*.

Friendship is always a personal, singular encounter. But it carries a vocation to blossom, to open up to all humanity.[15] All the more if the two friends are believers, truthful seekers of God their Creator. Friendship is a school of the universal. Trustful, comforting, reciprocal relationship with a friend can be this

---

[15] The experience of love bears its own kind of fruit, although marriage can certainly include friendship.

school's laboratory, for in the shared experience of friendship identities expand as one offers hospitality to otherness in the person of the friend. In friendship the capacity to love can develop and expand until it becomes universal, including even the presumed "enemy," who is, in fact, a "potential friend."

Related through his friend to an (eschatological) future of communion in God, De Chergé's awakened heart was able to find in ordinary relations—as long as they were open to this future—the taste of authentic spiritual friendship, the taste of God. However, the word "friendship" is not very frequent in his writings,[16] especially compared to his use of the word "brotherhood." Many times these two words appear as close as synonyms. In the Christian tradition, the language of brotherhood traditionally suggests the requirement of a universal extension of love (through will and reason, rather than in a sentimental sense—especially when it comes to enemies!). All people are created by the same unique God, and therefore are brothers and sisters of one other. But De Chergé stressed also the Christic dimension of this unity, as he said strikingly that in Jesus, the Word was made brother,[17] indicating that the Word of God entered into friendship with all people. De Chergé was able to experience this brotherhood/friendship in what he called the "existential dialogue" of an everyday life shared with simple people that was a foretaste, even an anticipation, of the communion of saints. Far

[16] Over the last five centuries, because of an excessive fear that friendship could lead to passionate exclusivity, Christian tradition and theology were often very opposed to close friendship among monks and other vowed religious. Because of a fear of what "particular friendships" could lead to, the ideal promoted was that of a rational (not emotional) universal love that extended even to the enemy. However, the early generation of the Cistercian branch of Christian monasticism (twelfth century) is characterized by experiences of and reflection upon friendship as an authentic spiritual gift, even a manifestation of the common vocation to love. Aelred of Rievaulx's well-known *On Spiritual Friendship* corresponded to the *De Amicitia* of Cicero.

[17] In French, "*Le Verbe s'est fait frère,*" paralleling John 1:14: "The Word was made flesh."

beyond Cicero's classical definition of friendship as mutual accord concerning things divine and human, orientation or openness to God became for De Chergé the true criterion of friendship. This way of understanding friendship implied an awareness that God takes the initiative, is the initiator and the "third partner" of this relationship, although, because of divine transcendence and immanence, God remains totally different from the two friends.[18] Brother Christophe says it beautifully: "There is someone between us. . . . It is He who is between the one and the other when they are friends."

The monks of Tibhirine were in harmony with their Cistercian monastic tradition and especially with Aelred of Rievaulx, the twelfth-century author of *On Spiritual Friendship*. Aelred argued that antiquity's insightful understanding of friendship had to be reinterpreted in the light shed by God's revelation: the plan of the Creator brought a depth and breadth, unimagined by the pagans.[19] Brother Christophe was, in fact, recalling Aelred when he dared to assert that "God is friendship,"[20] altering the famous statement of Saint John that "God is Love." Humanity was created to participate in God's friendship, and despite the selfish perversion of the human heart, God's saving grace opens the eschatological horizon of the communion of saints, where the "glue" of purified feelings (like joy and pleasure) will join the action of will and reason so that we may live a universal love. Loving one's enemies, so unnatural in this world, is a commandment of Jesus but cannot proceed from human feelings. The gift

[18] See Matthew 18:20: "For where two or three are gathered together in my name, there am I in the midst of them." Surprisingly, Christian reflection upon friendship has often forgotten this inspiring sentence of Jesus.

[19] Aelred quotes many passages from the works of Cicero but adapts them to Christian views. An appeal to morality is the first way he criticizes the old definition (two robbers can form a pair of "friends"). But his main point is God's role of Creator and Merciful Savior.

[20] Christophe quoted Aelred in his text/testimony of 1994. See *Aime jusqu'au bout du feu*, p. 108. Referring to Jesus as God's crucified Love, he even states, "It is a historical fact: God is friendship."

of friendship is seen here as a "school" (as Saint Benedict designates the monastery) in which we learn eternal and universal love in God over the course of our earthly pilgrimage.

Monastic Life in Dialogue: Islam as the Friend of Each Day

The monastic "school" at Tibhirine found great accord with its neighbors' practice of Islam. De Chergé, who had studied Islam and Arabic (most intensely during two years in Rome), was greatly disposed to search for harmonies between the two different traditions. He was not motivated by fear, which tries to negate differences and forge a superficial "concordance" between the two traditions. Rather, his was the humble posture of a man of desire, full of hope and thirsting for a Truth that is always greater than our thoughts, minds, and deeds. When he was elected prior in 1984 and placed in charge of the community, he knew that he was in need of the light of "the other" in order to enter more deeply into his own tradition, and then to go deeper still until he reached the depth where all paths merge into the mystery of God.

Two images from ordinary life symbolized this dialogue: the well and the ladder. De Chergé enjoyed the friendship of a young Muslim whom he helped on his spiritual journey. They spoke about their conversations as a time when they dug their well. Once De Chergé asked his friend somewhat provocatively, "What kind of water do you think we will find at the bottom of the well: Muslim water or Christian water?" His friend responded, both pained and amused: "You still don't know? What we will find is the water of God."

In Tibhirine, as in any monastic community, two or three hours each day were devoted to prayerful reading and meditation on the Holy Scriptures. De Chergé's knowledge of Arabic enabled him to engage in a "dialogical" practice of *lectio divina* by reading the Holy Qurʾan in "parallel" with the Bible. His friendship with Mohammad had grown into a friendship with Islam, and he referred to Islam's Holy Scripture as a "gift of God to nurture the taste of Him." He felt it was a part of his prophetic mission to offer hospitality to the Holy Qurʾan in his *lectio divina*, letting the echo of the Scripture of others make itself heard in his own as a pleading friend. And this form of dia-logue (i.e., sharing a common word) helped him to listen to the Word of God at a deeper level.

The traditional image of the spiritual ladder was one that De Chergé used quite naturally. He imagined a ladder where one side is Christianity/monasticism and the other is Islam, with both sides holding the many common rungs we need to climb: memory of God (*dhikr*), fasting, prayer, the spiritual pilgrimage, sharing with the poor, etc. But our traditions also cherish common values like obedience, trust, poverty of heart, humility, the spirit of childhood, as highways toward sanctity. Friendship also has a place on the list, even though it is not very high on the list in the Christian tradition. If we are to climb up the rungs of the spiritual ladder, mutual recognition is needed to keep them horizontal. Humble respect of the other's gift along with friendship for the other makes it far easier to climb the ladder.

The *Alawyy* Sufi had a slightly different understanding of the ladder image that was used to describe Tibhirine's experience of "monasticism in dialogue." They spoke of an A-shaped step ladder, where one side of the "A" is Islam and the other is Christianity. One side needs the other, otherwise one will never get off the ground. Climbing together, each rung brings one closer to the Muslim or Christian friend and closer to God. On this ladder each tradition maintains its own way of climbing the rungs, but is enriched by the other tradition's way of using the "tools of good works" as Saint Benedict calls them. We could easily add many of them to the above list: conversion of heart, a constant sense of the divine presence, trust in providence, the urgent need for boundless hospitality, the call to spiritual combat, etc. In all of them we see the action of the unique Spirit of holiness, whose "secret joy is always to establish communion and restore resemblance by playing with the differences," as De Chergé put it in his Testament.

A passage from the Qur'an expresses very well for De Chergé his own perception of Christian monasticism in dialogue:

> Had God willed, He could have made you one congregation. But He thus puts you to the test through the gifts He has given each of you. Vie then with one another in good works. To God is your final destiny—all of you—then He will inform you of everything you had disputed. (5:48)

This mutual emulation of good deeds is the "salt" of the encounter. It includes the necessity of duration, faithfulness, and perseverance. Friendship, a relationship that has God as its horizon, does not happen overnight, and De Chergé knew the Algerian proverb: "Two men can say they are friends only when they have together consumed a ton of salt."[21]

Thanks to a long and fruitful practice of existential dialogue (he did not have much time for the dead ends of "theological" dialogue), he was really committed to establishing connections between the constitutive elements of monastic life and the practice of Islam ('Arkân ad-dîn). Even the call of the muezzin was regarded by the monks as a call to prayer, a reminder of their vocation to live continually in the presence of God. In the last years, they would stop their liturgy as a sign of respect if the muezzin was calling.

The Friend of the Last Minute: A Responsibility for All

De Chergé's singular experience of friendship with Mohammad had definitively opened his heart, broken the "natural" barriers of mistrust and fear. His mystical awareness enabled him to live and relate with others at a level of depth, where humanity

---

[21] The image of salt in relationships is common to many cultures. Early in his spiritual journey, De Chergé quoted Aristotle: "People have to grind a lot of salt together to become friends."

is truly one, as it is in the eyes of God. But in the final years, as Algeria descended into an ever deeper spiral of violence, his prophetic hopes were sorely tried, as were the hopes of all people devoted to peace and friendship between religions. In the people of Algeria, it was humanity that was suffering violence. The time came for this friend of Islam to stand watch for the truth of Islam against its perversion, time to stand watch for humanity, in the name of those who "forgot" theirs by killing their brothers. And finally, the time came to follow Muhammad, to follow Jesus, in the "greater love." At its summit, friendship may well involve a rendezvous with death, because, as Brother Luc would say in a striking summing up of his hope, "Death is God."

The now well-known Testament of De Chergé can, in fact, be heard as the Testament of the whole community of Tibhirine. Through his teaching and example the prior certainly helped his brethren to be open to the otherness of Islam, as well as to overcome their sharp differences of temperament that at times had made community life quite explosive. The depth of communion they reached, which impressed all those who visited Tibhirine during the last two years, was clearly the work of God.

At the end of his Testament, De Chargé addresses his thanks to his friends from Algeria, including his possible murderer, whom he calls "the friend of the last minute":

> And you, the friend of the last minute, who won't have known what you were doing; Yes, for you also I want this MERCI, and this farewell foreseen by you. And may we be granted to meet again, happy thieves, in Paradise, if God wills, Father of both of us. Amen! *Insh'Allah!* [22]

---

[22] De Chergé speaks of an *A-Dieu* as he introduces his testament. The ordinary formulation would be *adieu* (meaning "farewell"), but he writes it as two words, which literally mean "(rendezvous)-by-God." And at the end, he repeats the word *A-Dieu*, but associates it with *MERCI*, meaning both "thank you" and "mercy," a reference to the All-Merciful, *El-Rahman*, whom he will encounter through death. The richness of the last sentence is even greater because of the allusion to Levinas, the Jewish philosopher, and his concept of *visage* (face). For him the human visage carries God's

The literary genius of the writer is obvious, but De Chergé's Testament is not just rhetoric or poetry, and this for several reasons. First of all, if we take seriously his conception of friendship as a gift of God and a call to greater intimacy with Him, he would owe his face-to-face encounter with God, his entry into the communion of saints, to this paradoxical "friend" who would cause his death. De Chergé once quoted this *hadîth* to the community: Abraham said to the Angel of Death: "Did you ever see a friend make his friend die?" And God revealed to him: "Did you ever see someone who loved disdain the encounter with the One he loves?"[23] And he writes in the Testament that God cannot be absent from this event, brutal though it may be. They [his community, church, and family] should accept that "the unique Master of all life could not be stranger to this brutal departure."

But De Chergé, along with his brother monks, also clearly said he did not wish that any human brother would be the author of his martyrdom, especially if it be an Algerian and a Muslim, who would murder in the name of a distorted image of a religion he respected and cherished.

We read in the Bible that the story of humanity after the creation of Adam and Eve started with violence: Cain murdered his brother Abel because his own offering had been disregarded by God, who accepted his brother's. Cain refused to obey God's call to dominate his violence and to be the safe-keeper of his brother. He murdered Abel, and by doing so "killed" the humanity (that subsisted) in both of them. De Chergé was inspired by the passage of the Qur'an referring to this story: "Whoever kills one

commandment "You shall not kill," which is the first step for human coexistence. De Chergé's offering of his life, in a Jesus-like way, "saves" the murderer from the consequences of his transgression. (We can think here of Louis Massignon and his interpretation of *Hallaj*', martyrdom.)

[23] See Aiguebelle's edition of De Chergé's talks to the community, *Dieu pour tout jour* (Abbaye Notre-Dame d'Aiguebelle, 2006), p. 111. The greater love is the threshold of the mystery where life and death are overcome. Therefore, in the Gospel of John, the cross of Jesus is also the throne of his glorification by God.

single man, if he is not guilty of murder, or sedition, is considered to have killed the whole humankind" (5:32).[24] And the following sentence is no less expressive: "Whoever has saved one single man is considered as if he had saved the whole humankind."

To be a friend of God implies becoming the brother and friend of all, responsible for their humanity, even if the price be one's life.[25] Looked at this way, hospitality in Tibhirine had reversed: men of peace, the monks had become the hosts of their neighbor's hope, hosts of their lives threatened by the surrounding folly of homicide.[26] De Chergé had come to accept his death long before he actually died: since he became a monk his life was already freely given, dedicated to God and the Algerian people. But he also felt that they had been entrusted with the mission of staying in solidarity with the people of Algeria, of standing watch to "save" the humanity of those who forgot theirs by violence and killings and in doing so distorted the true visage of God. He endeavored to see and protect in each human being, even those who had been led astray, the vestige of God, the hidden intimacy of God with all creatures. And he perfectly knew the price of this stance. By the time De Chergé was writing the end of his Testament, the "friend of the last minute" had for him

[24] The second category of exception (*fassâd*, sedition) can lead to several interpretations. There is a parallel tradition in the *Mishna* (*Sanhédrin*, 4,5).

[25] The monks called the Islamists "brothers of the mountain," and the government armed forces the "brothers of the plain." By using this terminology, they refused to take sides for one against the other, but rather freely chose to remain in brotherhood with both, refusing the law of violence they tried to impose. And Luke, the doctor, cured people without discrimination. It is worth noting that the Catholic religious murdered in Algeria were all persons of communion and not proselytes, people deeply involved in relationships of social support and friendship, with ordinary people. Radicals from the two sides of the conflict tried to impose the law of violence as the only "solution."

[26] An anecdote demonstrates this reversal of hospitality. As the community had to discern if they should stay or leave, De Chergé once told a neighbor they were like "birds on a branch." The neighbor answered: "But we are the birds, and you are the branch: if you depart, we have nowhere to go."

the visage of Sayah Attia, the "visitor" of Christmas night 1993 and author of more than one hundred deaths, who had promised to come back. This night he had managed to "disarm" the terrorist, by looking at him as a fellow human. Face-to-face, himself "disarmed," he had firmly resisted Sayah Attia's requests, addressing the man's faith and humanity that were deeper than his murderous deeds. He persevered afterward in calling him his friend, just as Jesus did not exclude from his friendship the disciple who was about to betray him during his last supper.

This leads to a third dimension of this "friendship of the last minute." In his Testament, De Chergé confesses himself to be a "thief," meaning by this that he had lived long enough to know that he too is an accomplice of evil and violence. But he also calls himself a "happy thief" because he confesses this in the light of divine mercy. If there were no conversion, then standing watch for all, hoping for every human in the name of God, would be mere idealism, a cheap dream.

In this Algerian tragedy, De Chergé recognized the dramatic opposition between Love and hatred, between Light and darkness, the frontline of which goes across the heart of each human being. Here is where the true *jihad* begins. By confessing the evil in his own heart as well as his complicity with it, De Chergé, a pure-hearted man if there ever was one, whose desire since childhood had been to serve God,[27] engaged in true solidarity with all humanity, including evildoers. He accepted the destiny of the righteous of all times who suffered persecution, and entered into the mystery of salvation of Jesus Christ. His relationship with his brother monks was a daily call to conversion from evil to God, from his own violence to peace, from his reflex of revenge to forgiveness. If not in fact, then in vocation and hope, the other, brother and friend, remains the road that leads to friendship with God and brings healing to the human heart.

---

[27] When he was eight years old, his grandfather found a piece of paper on which he had written "I shall be a priest."

Deeply affected by the atrocities that surrounded him, moved by compassion for his neighbors, feeling that his humanity, his faith and his hope were being beaten down, De Chergé repeated this prayer, addressed to the God of Peace: "Disarm me, Disarm us [monks], Disarm them [murderers of both sides]."

The Heritage of Seven Friends of God

The "excess of violence" between 1992 and 1996 became for the threatened monks a call to an "excess of love." The commandment of Jesus to love one's enemy appeared more urgent than ever. It called them to greater conversion, to purifying their hearts still prone to violence, to practicing gratuitous love, and to growing transparency to the Spirit of holiness. Brother Christophe, to whom this final section will give voice, put it this way: "Our prayer of beggars engages us more deeply in this mystery of friendship for the Glory of God and for the sake of the world. . . . This friendship (extended to all) is entrusted to us as a mission."

A man of great sensitivity (he fought against the violence of some of his reactions) and a true mystic, Christophe had also received the double gift of friendship and poetry. Early in his monastic life in France, he enjoyed deep, mystical friendships that lasted after his departure to Algeria and Tibhirine. Such friendships prepared him to open his heart to a horizon that included the Muslim friend, a horizon that was already De Chergé's. As the monk responsible for the garden, Brother Christophe's daily work with the monastery's associates blossomed as a mystical garden. Friendship was an epiphany of God in ordinary things. When he wrote about friendship—and he wrote a lot—his vision centered on Christ Jesus, the Friend par excellence, with whom Christophe felt so closely bound. One of his friends said that his love transformed him into the image of Christ, and therefore had to be fulfilled by the same kind of selfless gift of his life.

If De Chergé already inhabited a universal horizon of friendship, and was therefore at times hard to follow, Brother Christophe's gift reminds us how much the inner call to embrace everyone is anything but a synonym for indifference. Love always involves a preference, a choice. Friendship never dismisses the intensity of the particular on its way to the universal. Christophe interchanged the words brotherhood and friendship, probably because in French the verb *"aimer"* (to love) is so closely related to the noun *"ami"* (friend). "The friend is the brother reclaimed day after day. . . . In this way, friendship should be the core of a fraternal humanity." The order of the first sentence can also be reversed: the brother (as monks call each other) reclaimed day after day becomes as close as a friend (someone chosen, unlike a brother). When Brother Christoph wrote, "There is someone between us. . . . It is He who is between the one and the other when they are friends," he was speaking of his friendship with a monk from his previous community, but his words can also refer to the community of Tibhirine. For him, this "someone" is clearly Christ, the face of God, the face of his friendship. As a friend of Jesus, he felt commissioned to convey his love to everyone, adding, "To be a friend is a serious matter. It exceeds both of us. It makes us die. There is nothing left but the gift."

At the end of their community life in dialogue, the monks of Tibhirine, so close to martyrdom (but also so reluctant to apply this word to themselves), had reached the point where the last encounter was anticipated as a grace of God, foreseen by Him whose gift would pass through them.[28]

The fatal gesture of the "friend of the last minute" was foreseen by De Chergé as something that would make them two happy thieves. But the gift of God is always greater: the Testament of De Chergé was fulfilled by friendship, the loving unto death of the whole community. Beyond the two happy thieves, they have become, like Abraham, "a benediction for all nations," a sign of hope for the communion of religions that should bring peace to a world of violence. The gift of their lives has joined together the

---

[28] Alluding to his priesthood, Christophe wrote, "The gift of Jesus passes through my hands."

gift of Mohammad and the gift of Jesus in God and invites us to enter into the Greater Mystery, the mystery of friendship and love.

"Nothing is left but the gift." This is precisely what makes the Testament of Tibhirine so alive today. Because the gift of friendship is eternal, because it is God's gift, we are here invited to share it with one another.

The Qur'an's Multifaceted Picture of Muslim/Christian Relations

Maximilian (Fredrick) Musindai

Any open-hearted believer should have a deep desire for dialogue. Christians, walking in the footsteps of Jesus Christ, have had a long tradition of dialogue. Although Jesus said he was sent first of all to the "lost sheep of the house of Israel," he always sought to go beyond the barriers of social class, politics, or religion. He spoke with a Samaritan woman, listened to a Syrophoenician woman and granted her request, admired the faith of the Roman centurion, commended the repentance of the "men of Nineveh" and the wisdom of "the Queen of the South." A Christian approach to dialogue can be summed up in the words of the apostle Peter, who says, "Always be prepared to make a defense to any who calls you to account for the hope that is in you, yet do it with gentleness and reverence; and keep your conscience clear" (1 Pet 3:15-16).

For their part, Muslims understand well the message of the noble Qur'an inviting them to dialogue with the believers who were their associates from the very beginning, "Dispute not with the People of the Book save in the fairer manner" (29:46). The Prophet Muhammad was asked to "Call thou (People) to the way of thy Lord with wisdom and good admonition and dispute with them in the better way" (16:125).[1]

---

[1] Pontifical Council for Interreligious Dialogue, *Guidelines for Dialogue between Christians and Muslims*, Interreligious Documents vol. 1, prep.

What especially caught my attention in the Qur'an with regard to the relationship between Islam and Christianity was a relative tolerance, openly declared, which gave Christianity a special rank among the "People of the Book." It is well known that Islam extends to the People of the Book in general a warm invitation to come to a common statement of belief: "Say, People of the Book! Come now to a word common between us and you, that we serve none but God, and that we associate not aught with Him, and do not some of us take others as Lords, apart from God" (3:64).

The relations of Muhammad and of the first Muslims with the Christians were good on the whole.[2] As compared with the Jews, Christians were to be treated with great friendliness, as it is said in the noble Qur'an:

> Thou wilt surely find the most hostile of men to the believers are the Jews and the idolaters; and thou will surely find the nearest of them in love to the believers are those who say "We are Christians"; that, because some of them are priests and monks, and they wax not proud, and when they hear what has been sent down to the Messenger, thou seest their eyes overflow with tears because of the truth they recognize. They say, "Our Lord, we believe: so do thou write us down among the witness." (5:82f.)

> And We sent Noah, and Abraham, and We appointed the Prophecy and the Book to be among their seed; and some of them are guided, and many of them are ungodly. Then We sent, following in their footsteps, Our Messengers; and We sent, following Jesus son of Mary, and gave unto Him the Gospel. And We set in the hearts of those who followed Him tenderness and mercy." (57:26f.)

Any attempt to study the relationships between Islam and Christianity, or between Muslims and Christians, must go back

---

Maurice Borrmans, trans. Marston R. Speight (New York: Paulist Press, 1981), p. 28.

[2] Saad Ghrab, "Islam and Christianity: From Opposition to Dialogue," *Islamo-Christiana* 13 (1985): 99–100.

to the earliest experiences that Muhammad himself had with Christians.

This task is made difficult for a number of reasons. First of all, the religious panorama of the Arabian Peninsula before Islam is quite complex. Arabia was home to many forms of religions and sects, Christian[3] as well as others. What type of Christians did the Prophet know? Secondly, little documentation is available about Muhammad's activities before his prophetic ministry. As for the Qur'an, it portrays changing attitudes toward the "People of the Book" without explaining why attitudes changed.

Contacts with Christians before the Revelation

Muhammad was born about 570 CE. His father died near the time of his birth, and he lost his mother when he was six. He was cared for briefly by his grandfather and then raised by Abu Talib, his uncle, who was a trader and head of the prominent Hashim clan in Mecca.

In the closing decades of the sixth century, a thriving trade network spread from Saudi Arabia north to Syria, east as far as India, and into northern Africa. Early Muslim histories report that Muhammad travelled with his uncle on trading journeys as far as Syria. It is believed that, given his work as a business-man who moved hundreds of kilometers with caravans, Muhammad must have had informal contacts with individual

---

[3] There were Christians in the Arabian Peninsula before the dawn of Islam. In the northwest, toward Mesopotamia, lived Arab tribes that were partly Christian. In the south (Yemen) there was a large Christian presence. At the center of the peninsula, Christians were few and scattered, in contrast to the large communities of Jews, for example, in Medina. It remains difficult to understand the type of Christianity that each community identified itself with. Many who were judged to be heretics had taken refuge in the area to escape persecution. What is certain is that Arabia was far from the important theological centers of the time and that the Christians themselves were quite divided.

Christians. In Islamic tradition, the most important of these contacts were with two persons.

The first was Bahira.[4] He is said to have been a Christian monk in Bosra (Syria). Some sources identify him as a Nestorian Christian. There are different traditions (one by Ibn Hisham, another by Ibn Sa'd, and another by Al-Tabari) regarding the encounter between Muhammad and Bahira). When he was a young boy, nine to twelve years old, Muhammad went on a trade journey with Abu Talib. He met this monk who revealed to him his prophetic destiny, telling the young Muhammad that he would become an important Prophet. One tradition attests that this monk saw some sign in the boy himself to indicate that he would be a Prophet; another holds that the monk saw a cloud over the boy and a branch of a tree giving him a shade, regardless of the position of the sun. Later Muslims have tended to take all traditions about the event as complementing one another. The hermit is supposed to have told Abu Talib (Abu Bakr in another tradition) what he had seen and asked him to take good care of the boy lest the Jews (according to Ibn Sa'd) or Rum/Byzantines (according to Al-Tabari), do him harm.

A myth has been added affirming that the monk knew Muhammad because he found his coming mentioned in some authentic Christian Books (Gospels) that were in his possession.

Is Bahira a historical person? We have no proof about that. What is sure is that an ancient tradition holds that a Christian monk predicted that Muhammad was destined to be a Prophet. Is there a polemical influence behind this tradition? It is not clear, but the tradition's statement that the Prophet was twelve years old when he met Bahira may be intended to call to mind the twelve years attributed to Jesus when he held a discussion with the doctors of law (Luke 2:42-49). Early Christian polemics have painted Bahira as a heretic monk who inspired Muhammad.

---

[4] See Armand Abel, "Bahira," in *Encyclopedia of Islam*, vol. 1 (Leiden, Netherlands: Brill Academic, 2002) , p. 922.

The second Christian with whom Muhammad had important contacts was Waraqa ibn Nawfal.[5] Waraqa ibn Nawfal was a cousin of Muhammad's wife, Khadija, and some traditions go so far as to affirm that he had proposed to marry her. For some unknown reason the marriage never took place, but they remained close. Waraqa ibn Nawfal was not only a *hanif*,[6] but had also converted to Christianity. He is said to have "studied" under the people of the Gospel and the Torah. He could write both in Arabic and Hebrew. He is the person who confirmed Muhammad in his prophetic call when, after the Prophet had his first vision, Waraqa said, "There has come to him the greatest law that came to Moses; surely he is the Prophet of his people."

Not much is known about the life of Waraqa, although some Muslim traditions count him among the first companions of the Prophet (*Sahaba*). What is commonly believed is that he retained his Christian faith.

Meccan Period

There were Christians in Mecca,[7] isolated individuals living as traders and slaves. Certain elements of Christianity were also circulating in society. For example, the Qur'an contains apocryphal stories about Jesus and Mary and ideas of judgment day, the hereafter, and angels. There is no indication that the Prophet was in touch with a well-formed Christian community or church. Nevertheless, much of what is known about the Meccan period, especially from the Qur'anic verses of the time, shows a rather friendly attitude of the Prophet toward the People of the Book in general (Jews and Christians), whom it refers to as "believers"

[5] Ibid.

[6] A term for a person who, during the period known as the Pre-Islamic period or "Age of Innocence," rejected idolatry and retained some or all of the tenets of the religion of Abraham.

[7] Christian residents in Mecca were few. See Montgomery Watt, *Muhammad's Mecca* (Edinburgh: University Press, 1988), p. 36.

(85:4-8). It also says, "Those who doubt should consult those who read the scriptures revealed before Muhammad" (21:7; 16:43; 10:94).

The reason Muhammad did not encounter a community of well-formed Christians may be that, as already noted, Christians in the Hijaz were few and scattered. Or it may have been that the Prophet met Christians, but did not have a deep knowledge of who they were and what they believed in. Having felt called to be a Prophet, Muhammad must have expected to be readily accepted by Jews and Christians. The fact that he was not, and his increasing awareness of their own internal divisions, must have left a negative impact on Muhammad (23:52f.; 21:92f.).

Muslims in Abyssinia

Because of persecution in Mecca, Muhammad first sent a group of his followers to Abyssinia (modern-day Ethiopia). They included Uthman ibn Affan, a future Caliph of the Muslims, his wife, Ruqayya, and Zubayr ibn al-Awwam, a cousin of the Prophet. The Prophet appointed Uthman ibn Mazun, one of his principal companions, as leader of this group.

The first migration took place around the fifth year of his ministry, in 615 CE. Negus, the king of Abyssinia, welcomed the Muslim refugees from Mecca into his kingdom.[8] He gave them sanctuary, and they enjoyed peace, security, and freedom of worship. About a year later, the Muslims in Abyssinia heard rumors that the Quraysh tribe in Mecca had accepted Islam. If that was true, then there was no reason for them to live in exile. They were homesick and so decided to return to Mecca. But on their arrival at Mecca, they found out that the rumors they heard were false. In fact, the Quraysh had stepped up its persecution of Muslims. They therefore left Mecca once again, taking many other Muslims with them. This new group comprised eighty-three men and

---

[8] Ghrab, "Islam and Christianity," p. 100.

eighteen women. Muhammad appointed his first cousin, Ja'affar ibn Abi Talib, an elder brother of Ali, as leader of the group.

The second migration of Muslims to Abyssinia took place in the sixth year of the Muhammad's mission, which corresponds to the year 616 CE. They were received by King Negus, the Christian king of Abyssinia. What this implies is that Muhammad, or at least some one among the converts, had links in the court of King Negus. The Prophet himself may not have had direct contact with the king, but the fact that his community was received there may point to some indirect contacts between him and the court of King Negus. The fact that Muslims were protected by the Christians of Ethiopia meant that Christians would, for a time, not be targeted as such by Muhammad.

The Medina Period

The dominant theme here is the deteriorating relationship between the Muslims and the Jewish population of Medina (Q. 2:40-150). In the later Medina period, there will be indications of contact with Christians. While we cannot give a precise account of the nature of these contacts, what we discover in the Qur'an is a change in attitude toward Christians and Jews: like the Jews, Christians arrogantly believe that only they will go to paradise (2:111, 120, 135); Christians are accused of calling themselves God's children (5:18); they are divided (5:14); they are opposed to the message brought by the Prophet (9:32f.); some of their doctrines are seen by the Prophet as "unbelief" (*kufur*) and idolatry (*shirk*); God never commanded monasticism (57:27), but they take monks as lords (9:34f.); Christians and Jews should not be taken as allies (*awliya*) (5:51); they are to be fought until they are humbled and pay *jizya* (9:29).

Another Picture of Christians

We also find in the Qur'an a positive portrayal of monasticism (3:113-115; 22:40; 5:82; 24:36-38); an acknowledgement that Allah has put tenderness and mercy in the hearts of those who follow Jesus (57:27); and a presentation of Christians in a more positive light than Jews (5:82). And yet, although there are verses that are more positive toward Christians than toward Jews, it is likely that the bad relationships between Jews and the Prophet also affected his attitude toward Christians.

While there are verses that make reference to Jesus, this does not necessarily imply a positive attitude toward Christians themselves. Jesus is referred to as a Prophet before The Prophet, since the latter had to be, according to the message he received, the last of the biblical prophets.

The Delegation from Najiran

In 632 CE, after conquering many tribes, Muhammad received in Medina a Christian delegation from Najiran. A theological dispute between these Christians and the Prophet led the two parties to have recourse to the so-called *Mubahala,* an oath in which one calls a curse upon himself if he is lying. The Najirans were called to this by Muhammad, but they hesitated. Afterward they opted for a treaty of friendship and nonaggression with the Prophet.[9]

Contacts with the Byzantines

The Byzantines and the Persians were the two super powers in the region at the time of Muhammad. Because of the constant fighting between these two powers, they were getting weaker at the time Muhammad began his territorial expansion campaigns.

Traditional Islamic sources hold that in 628 CE, the Prophet sent a letter to the Byzantine emperor Heraclius, inviting him to convert to Islam. Ibn Ishaq and other Muslim historians record that sometime between February 628 and 630 CE, Muhammad

[9] See Ghrab, "Islam and Christianity," pp. 100f.

also sent out letters to Arabian and non-Arabian leaders. For example, he entrusted Hatib ibn Abi Baittah with a letter to al-Muqawqis, "ruler of Alexandria." Al-Muqawqis replied by sending Muhammad, as a gift, four slave girls, one of whom was Mary (Mariah), mother of Ibrahim, the only son of Muhammad, who died at a tender age. In Islamic tradition, al-Muqawqis is identified as Bishop (or Patriarch) Cyrus of Alexandria, who administered Egypt on behalf of the Byzantine Empire.[10]

A Worsening of Relations

It appears that the attitude of Muhammad toward Christians changed from one of sympathy to opposition. There are several possible explanations for this.

As has already been noted, there existed different theological streams of Christianity in Arabia. It is likely that adherents of these different streams responded differently to Muhammad and are thus praised or criticized by the noble Qur'an accordingly.

There was also a chronological progression in Muhammad's attitude toward Christians: from sympathy, to conflict, and finally, to a total breakdown of relations. Given that the Prophet was sure of the support of the People of the Book at the beginning of his ministry, he could not but be positive toward them. When they showed themselves reluctant to accept him, his attitude toward them must have changed. Positive verses about

---

[10] There are reasons to doubt this. It was after Heraclius's capture of Egypt from the Sassanid Persians that Cyrus succeeded to the see of Alexandria (630 CE). It is unlikely that a Christian bishop would send slave girls as gifts to a non-Christian ruler. While al-Muqawqis, in his letter of reply, affirms that he believed in the coming of a prophet, what he may mean by this is that Christians believe in the Second Coming of Christ. It is unlikely that it was a Christian bishop who affirmed the coming of another prophet. There is reason to believe that while the contact with an Alexandrian ruler is plausible, the latter was no more than a Persian governor and not a Christian bishop.

Christians would thus refer to Christians who at some stage acknowledged the divine origin of Qur²an (5:82-85 and 3:119).

Another explanation for the worsening of relations is that during the period of expansion to the North (the Medina period), Muhammad was opposed by tribes who were mainly Christian and defended the Byzantine Empire.

From the beginning of his prophetic mission, Muhammad was convinced that his was a continuation of the mission of the biblical prophets. He also believed that Christians would be able and willing to accept his message. His "ideal" Christian community collided with the Christian communities actually in existence, provoking ups and downs in the attitude of the Prophet toward Christians.

We have seen that while the Prophet met some Christians, he probably did not have extensive knowledge of Christian doctrine. However, what he transmits to his followers about Christians and Christianity is, within Islam, held to be divinely revealed. This belief may make it difficult for a Muslim to be receptive to what the Christian of today has to say about his or her identity and faith.

Even though we may find that Muhammad had various contacts with Christians, Muslims would not accept this to mean that Christianity had some influence on Islam. Therefore, just as some early Christians affirmed the prophetic nature of Muhammad, so the Christians of today are also expected to accept it.

A confusion of Christian theologies and doctrines leads to a wrong understanding of Christianity. Disunity among Christians, especially on doctrinal issues, has been and still continues to be a stumbling block to dialogue with other religions.

The Monastic/Shi²a Interreligious Dialogue

The encounter between Abbot Timothy Wright and Dr. Mohammad Ali Shomali may be seen as heralding a new dawn in the search for Christian/Muslim dialogue. Dr. Shomali himself has written,

I later visited Ampleforth Abbey in north Yorkshire and stayed there overnight. I attended their offices of prayer, met and talked to many monks and was impressed by the openness and hospitality of the Abbot, Timothy Wright. . . . Later when we became close friends, he told me that when I was visiting them he himself was worried what "this smiling face" would do there. Indeed, that was the first encounter of the brethren with a Muslim scholar.

The journey continued. In the next couple of years, I spent time and energy exploring the Christian world. I visited many places in different countries and within the UK. God gifted me many good friends. After several visits of the community in Ampleforth and before my return home, I invited Abbot Timothy and one of the young monks to visit us in Qum. We had fruitful meetings and discussions and their talks were welcomed by the seminarians there.

A turning point. As planned during their stay in Qum, and with the later involvement of Heythrop College, University of London, the first Catholic-Shiʿa conference was held in July 2003.[11]

Conclusion

Prior to the events of September 11, 2001, the media mainly portrayed two kinds of Muslims: rich oil princes and poor unemployed Muslims in the streets of Arab cities. The common wisdom was and still is that we must give ear to Muslims in Arab streets, since their voice shapes political consciousness in those societies. However, in many Arab and Muslim nations, the street counts almost for nothing, which is the main reason people often crowd it yelling hateful slogans.

We have a lot to learn about Islam, but to do so we have to go beyond the oil princes and the street protesters. We need to find

[11] Anthony O'Mahony, Wulstan Peterburs, and Muhammad Ali Shomali, eds., *Catholic and Shiʿa Dialogue: Studies in Theology and Spirituality* (London: Melisende, 2011), pp. 6–7.

out who to give ear to if we genuinely desire to improve our relations with the Muslim world and prevent the ever-escalating misunderstanding that leads to hostility. Mainstream Islam restored to its past glory, traditional and pluralistic in nature, will lead to a new, fruitful contribution to a sane humanity. It will draw on the hidden rich history we have neglected for many centuries, blinded by prejudice, myth, and fear. It is imperative that we find reliable Muslim allies in this struggle, that we endeavor to learn their languages and understand their cultural differences as well as their similarities. If indeed Islam were an inherently violent and aggressive religion, as it is so often wrongly portrayed in the media, it would by now be something only found in history books, as in the case with numerous pagan cults.[12]

---

[12] Jason Burke, *Al-Qaeda: The True Story of Radical Islam* (Harlow, UK: Penguin Books, 2004), p. 48.

Friends and Friendship in Biblical Literature

Timothy Wright, OSB

Friendship is an inherently difficult topic for an interreligious dialogue because the word "friend" is not itself a religious or theological concept. Friendship refers to a certain kind of relationship between people in a society, religious or not. A friend has been defined as one "joined to another in mutual benevolence and intimacy,"[1] or "one attached to another by affection, loyalty or common experience."[2] A friend is outside the family, shares common interests, and can be in a relationship of loving intimacy. Significantly, these definitions make no mention of friendship with God, but that is a legitimate use of the word, and an especially important one in the context of this essay.

"Friendship" as it is presented in our two inspired Scriptures can be considered from three different vantage points: first, the friendship believers have with God; second, the special friendship that exists between believers of the same faith who see in each other the revelation of the presence of God; and third, the possibility of friendship between adherents of different faiths

---

[1] *Oxford English Dictionary*, s.v. "friend."

[2] Louise Marlow, "Friendship and Friend in the Qurʾan," in *Encyclopedia of the Qurʾān*, ed. Jane Dammen McAuliffe *et al.* (Leiden Belgium: Brill Academic), CD-ROM edition.

who see in the "other" a real presence of God, but one that is differently understood and expressed. The extent of the difference will vary because holiness and sinfulness are not limited by boundaries of revealed faith.

Before beginning a consideration of some of the biblical passages that highlight friendship, a word about the significantly different ways Muslims and Christians understand was is meant by the "inspiration" of our Scriptures. For Muslims, the Qur'an is literally God speaking; it is God's message at its highest magnification. For Christians, the Bible is the Word of God communicated through human authors writing under divine inspiration. Both accept divine inspiration; each interprets it differently. For Muslims, Arabic is the language of God. For Christians, the inspiration of God is more diffused, across time, style, and textual groupings. Different languages, diverse cultures, and changing historical situations have each had an effect on the biblical text— hence the need for critical study to understand its message.

A Brief Overview of Friendship in the Bible and the Qur'an

The *Collegeville Pastoral Dictionary of Biblical Theology* summarizes the biblical view: "The Bible touches on friendship mainly in passing, without extended investigation or reflection." [3] In the eight English translations of the Qur'an consulted, half include "friend" and/or "friendship" in their index (Dawood, Pickthall, Yusuf Ali, and Ali Quli Qara'i) and half do not (Shakir, Maulana Muhammad Ali, Abdel Haleem and Muhammad Asad). The most important kind of friendship is friendship with God, as is clearly stated in the *Encyclopaedia of the Qur'an*: "The Qur'an repeatedly pronounces God, from whose will there is no escape, as the only friend and helper of the believers [see 4:45,

---

[3] Joseph Jensen, "Friendship," in *The Collegeville Pastoral Dictionary of Biblical Theology*, ed. Carroll Stuhlmueller (Collegeville, MN: Liturgical Press, 1994), p. 348.

9:116, 29:22; 33:17, 42:31; 2:257; 3:68; 5:55-56; 6:127; 7:155; 18:26];
according to most interpretations, these passages represent calls
to communal solidarity and activism among believers."[4]

One can conclude that the One God is the inspiration behind
these inspired texts, but the notion of friendship is portrayed in
each in different ways, more complementary than opposing.

Muslims and Christians can trace the origin of friendship to
the first couple. Adam and Eve reveal a capacity to enjoy life in
Paradise, an ability to communicate with each other, a freedom
to make choices, and a weakness to be tempted to disobedience.
In the moment of disobedience, the two became aware that
something had changed. They asked questions of themselves,
faced examination by God, and suffered the consequences of
their action—expulsion from Paradise. At this point an important difference emerges: the Bible has Adam and Eve banished
to a life of hardship they could not escape. They could only
dream about the possibility of divine rescue. Muslims, however,
believe that Adam recognized his sin, repented, and was forgiven by God.

The Judeo-Christian tradition emphasizes the human ten-
dency to self-deification, which stands in the way of friendship
between God and human beings. The emphasis in the Muslim
tradition is on repentance and sorrow, which brings out the best
in God, whose nature is to be merciful and forgive, and who
reestablishes friendship.

Human friendship and divine friendship are closely related:
for Muslims, the presence of God is alive in the other and obliges
respect and kindness. For Christians, the Christ event opened up
new horizons through the indwelling of the risen Christ, empow-
ering them to be partners in the saving work of God. But in both
cases individuals still have free choice and take responsibility for
their own behavior in relationship to their neighbor.

---

[4] Marlow, "Friendship and Friend."

Examples of Friendship in the Bible

The story of the tower of Babel in Genesis 11 describes a people united in language and vocabulary who seek to ensure that the evil of "difference" would never threaten their existence. "Then they said, 'Come, let us build ourselves a city, and a tower with its top in the heavens, and let us make a name for ourselves; otherwise we shall be scattered abroad upon the face of the whole earth'" (4). God saw this as a threat to the divine plan and introduced multiple languages. One interpretation—but an unlikely one—is that different languages ensured that people were scattered according to language and thus were unable to develop human friendships from becoming so strong that they excluded God.

Division among people actually highlights the importance of friendship. One illustration of this is the friendship of Moses with Jethro and Joshua. Moses' relationship with Jethro was not just "professional." Jethro was more than an employer: his daughters became Moses' wives, and later he became an important adviser. Joshua, the divinely chosen successor, was always supportive of Moses, especially in challenging moments of rebellion. But perhaps most significant was his positive report about the "new land"; the reports of all the other scouts were negative. Joshua succeeded Moses as leader, entrusted with the task of settling into this new land.

A more powerful example of friendship between different peoples is that of Naomi, the widow whose sons died in Moab, and Ruth, the Moabite widow of one of those sons. When advised that her mother-in-law was returning home to Bethlehem, Ruth said she would accompany her. Naomi tried to persuade her against this, fearing that she would face an unknown future among a hostile people. Ruth persisted with these remarkable words that testify to friendship stretching across tribe and religion:

> Where you go, I will go;
> Where you lodge, I will lodge;
> your people shall be my people,
> and your God, my God.

> Where you die, I will die—
> there will I be buried.
> May the LORD do thus and so to me,
> and more as well,
> if even death parts me from you! (Ruth 1:16b-17)

Later, Ruth married again and became the great-grandmother of David and an ancestor of Jesus.

David, King of Judah not only had a large family from many wives, but also many friends. His closest friend was Jonathan, Saul's son:

> When David had finished speaking to Saul, the soul of Jonathan was bound to the soul of David, and Jonathan loved him as his own soul. . . . Then Jonathan made a covenant with David, because he loved him as his own soul. . . . Then Jonathan said to David, "Go in peace, since both of us have sworn in the name of the LORD, saying, 'The LORD shall be between my descendants and your descendants, forever.'" (1 Sam 18:1, 3; 20:42)

Another friend of a sort was Achish, King of Gath, ally of the Philistines, the archenemy of Israel. He gave the much-feared David not only refuge from Saul, but also a role in his army. However, he spared him from having to fight against his own people (1 Sam 27; 29).

One of the most moving biblical stories of friendship is that of the unnamed daughter of Jephthah. Jephthah was a rogue believer who parted company with the chosen people in the time of the Judges, only to be called back because of his success as a military leader. A rash vow to God, made when he doubted his ability to win battles, led to victory and the carrying out of the vow: the sacrifice of his only child, a daughter. She asks Jephthah, "Grant me one request. Give me two months to roam the hills and weep with my friends because I will never marry" (Judg 11:23, NIV). She accepted her vocation and died a martyr to a rash vow, without an heir, but with the memory of a happy time with her friends.

One who suffered the pain of opposition from friends was the prophet Jeremiah, for whom the whole network of friendship had eroded as the people abandoned the covenant and faced divine retribution. This is how he expressed his anger at the rejection of the Mosaic Law:

> Let each be on his guard against his friend; do not trust a brother; for every brother aims but to supplant and every friend is a peddler of slander. Each one cheats his friend, never telling the truth; they have trained their tongues to lie and devote all their energies to doing wrong. You live in a world of bad faith! Out of bad faith, they refuse to know me, Yahweh declares. (Jer 9:3-5, NJV)

The biblical presentation of friendship can be summarized under three headings: command, revelation and strength.

Command

> [Y]ou shall love your neighbor as yourself; I am the LORD. . . . When an alien resides with you in your land, you shall not oppress the alien. The alien who resides with you shall be to you as the citizen among you; you shall love the alien as yourself, for you were aliens in the land of Egypt: I am the LORD your God. (Lev 19:18b, 33-34)

Revelation

> Then God said, 'Let us make humankind in our image, according to our likeness. . . . So God created humankind in his image, in the image of God he created them; male and female he created them. (Gen 1:26-27)

Strength

> Set me as a seal upon your heart, as a seal upon your arm; for love is strong as death, passion fierce as the grave. Its flashes are flashes of fire, a raging flame. Many waters cannot quench love, neither can floods drown it. If one offered for love all the wealth of his house, it would be utterly scorned. (Song 8:6-7)

The most developed and systematic presentation of friendship in biblical literature is that found in Ben Sira, also known as Ecclesiasticus:

> Pleasant speech multiplies friends, and a gracious tongue multiplies courtesies. Let those who are friendly with you be many, but let your advisers be one in a thousand. When you gain friends, gain them through testing, and do not trust them hastily. For there are friends who are such when it suits them, but they will not stand by you in time of trouble. And there are friends who change into enemies, and tell of the quarrel to your disgrace. And there are friends who sit at your table, but they will not stand by you in time of trouble. When you are prosperous, they become your second self, and lord it over your servants; but if you are brought low, they turn against you, and hide themselves from you. Keep away from your enemies, and be on guard with your friends. Faithful friends are a sturdy shelter: whoever finds one has found a treasure. Faithful friends are beyond price; no amount can balance their worth. Faithful friends are life-saving medicine; and those who fear the Lord will find them. Those who fear the Lord direct their friendship aright, for as they are, so are their neighbors also. (6:5-17)

Human beings should be enhanced through friendship. With time, generosity, and faith in God, friendship grows ever deeper.[5]

The gospels show Jesus had little difficulty making friends. He was also the one who broke down barriers of race and religion. The recorded miracles include people of different ages, nationalities, and religions. They showed how easy it was to activate the healing ministry of Jesus, itself a sign of empathic friendship that provided a way into deeper issues relating to the

---

[5] For those interested, there are additional comments on friendship in Psalms 41:4-6; 88:18; 109:4; and 119:63. Isaiah 5:1-6 is a charming song of God's love. Other comments can be found in Proverbs 18:24 and 19:4, 6; and in Ecclesisasticus [Ben Sira] 6:5, 16; 12:8-9; 22:19-26.

meaning of life, the possibility of life after death, and moral behavior consonant with committed faith.

The Echo of Four Friendships as Portrayed in the Bible and the Qur'an

In both the Bible and the Qur'an, four individuals appear whose lives further illustrate the meaning of friendship: Abraham, Jonah, Job, and Joseph.

Abraham, "Friend of God"

Abraham occupies a key position in the inspired Scriptures of both Christians and Muslims. It is not without significance that he is named in both as "the friend of God." Reuven Firestone comments, "His qur'ānic appellation as [God's] friend (*khalīl*) in Q 4:125 formed the basis of his honorific title "Friend of God" (*khalīl Allāh*) in the Islamic tradition."[6]

The New Testament author James, quoting Genesis 15:6, writes, "Thus the scripture was fulfilled that says, 'Abraham believed God, and it was reckoned to him as righteousness,' and he was called the friend of God."

In the Qur'an 4:125 we read, "And who has a better religion than him who submits his will to Allah, being virtuous, and follows the creed of Abraham a *hanif*. And Allah took Abraham for a dedicated friend."

The similar language of friendship points to the unique relationship Abraham had with God. Touched by the call of God, Abraham was inspired to leave home, challenge his family to abandon their idols, entertain divine guests, obey the command of God with regard to the life of his son, rebuild the Kaba'a as a center for prayer, and be an example of faith and prayer in the One God

---

[6] See "Abraham" in the *Encyclopaedia of the Qur'an*, ed. Jane Dammen McAuliffe (Leiden, Netherlands: Brill Academic 2001–2006).

who gifted him with inner freedom. This is surely a clear sign of unique friendship with God. It is also a witness to what God can give to all believers who seek this friendship by repenting their sin, which is then confirmed by divine forgiveness.

Jonah/Dhu al-Nun and God

Another complex friendship described in the Hebrew Scriptures was that of God and the Prophet Jonah. Jonah was a rebel with a rigid, fundamentalist theology, whose self-will was stronger than the divine command. He only came to his senses when he ended up in the belly of the whale and prayed.[7] He prayed so effectively that he was rescued from this "exile" and proceeded to carry out the will of God. But he did it without much enthusiasm: his fundamentalism prevented that from happening. In spite of his conviction that the Ninevites were unworthy of forgiveness, his preaching was hugely successful. Ironically, this made him even more unhappy. We might wonder if such evil people would ever be pardoned by anyone, least of all the God whom they had so maligned! Although God continued to treat Jonah as a friend, the reader of the book of Jonah is left with the impression that this friendship did little to change Jonah's theology!

The story of Jonah in the Qur³an is quite similar to the biblical account, as the following summary makes clear: "Jonah, also called Dhū l-Nūn ("the man of the whale"), rebelled against God's mission, ran away in wrath, was swallowed by the fish, praised God, confessed his sin in the belly of the fish, and was thrown ashore (21:87-8). This and the rest of the story is told in 37:139-48: When he was saved, he found shade under a tree, and was sent "to a hundred thousand or more." In 68:48-50, Muhammad is admonished to wait with patience for the command of the Lord, and not to behave like "the man of the fish . . . who went away without God's permission."[8]

---

[7] Suras 10:98; 21:87-88; 27:139-148; 68:48; and Jonah 1–4.

[8] Heribert Busse, "Jonah" in the *Encyclopaedia of the Qur³an*.

The Muslim version has variants which make it more difficult to evaluate the degree of friendship Jonah had with God. What is common to both (and of greater importance), is the sense of a deep commitment to God. Jonah's anger may appear disrespectful to the reader, but it also illustrates the complexity contained in a relationship of faith, where, from an earthly perspective all the signs point in one direction, the divine decree seems to be moving in an opposite direction. This friendship of opposites is deeply reassuring for those perplexed by the sheer quantity of evil perpetrated by people who call themselves friends of God. Jonah must surely be their patron saint.

Job

The story of Job is similar in both Scriptures: a good man suddenly reduced to penury without any clear reason.[9]

In the biblical book of Job, his three friends try to persuade him that he should admit his sin because God does not punish the innocent. Job cries, "He has put my family far from me, and my acquaintances are wholly estranged from me. My relatives and my close friends have failed me. . . . All my intimate friends abhor me, and those whom I loved have turned against me" (19:13-14a, 19). In this difficult state, Job's faith was tested to the limit. He became angry with God, but never abandoned his faith. At the end God said to Eliphaz the Temanite, one of the three friends of Job, "My wrath is kindled against you and against your two friends; for you have not spoken of me what is right, as my servant Job has. . . . I will accept his prayer not to deal with you according to your folly; for you have not spoken of me what is right, as my servant Job has done" (42:7-8). It is precisely this divine capacity to absorb human anger that makes this story so compelling for Christians.

The Qur'anic version commends Job for his faith and patience and recognizes that God rewarded his endurance and restored

---

[9] Suras 21:73-74 and 38:41-44, and the book of Job.

his family as an example of how God might treat the faithful people.

Joseph and Pharaoh

In the story of Joseph, found both in the book of Genesis and the Qurʾan, the abused and rejected brother became not just a trusted official, but also Pharaoh's friend, as shown by his rapid promotion to second-in command in the Kingdom.[10] Pharaoh's generosity toward Joseph's family laid the foundation for the later escape of the Israelites from Egypt,[11] a friendship within a bigger divine plan.

Jesus' Dramatic Teaching on Friendship

There is one statement of Jesus that offers a unique challenge to Christians and Muslims alike. Because of its clarity, it cuts across all other statements from inspired Scripture:

> You have heard that it was said, "You shall love your neighbor and hate your enemy." But I say to you, Love your enemies and pray for those who persecute you, so that you may be children of your Father in heaven; for he makes his sun rise on the evil and on the good, and sends rain on the righteous and on the unrighteous. For if you love those who love you, what reward do you have? Do not even the tax collectors do the same? And if you greet only your brothers and sisters, what more are you doing than others? Do not even the Gentiles do the same? Be perfect, therefore, as your heavenly Father is perfect. (Matt 5:43-48)[12]

The words of Jesus go against every natural inclination and authoritative advice on how to treat the enemy and beyond all

---

[10] Sura 12 and Gen 41:37-45.

[11] See Gen 41ff. and Sura 12.

[12] The version in Luke is equally powerful; see Luke 6:27-36.

categories of tribal, national, and religious behavior. It requires a level of personal detachment, courage to take the first step, and the willingness to accept consequences that may not be intended.

Paul later expanded on these words of Jesus when he wrote,

> Beloved, never avenge yourselves, but leave room for the wrath of God; for it is written, "Vengeance is mine, I will repay, says the Lord." No, "if your enemies are hungry, feed them; if they are thirsty, give them something to drink; for by doing this you will heap burning coals on their heads." Do not be overcome by evil, but overcome evil with good. (Rom 12:19-21)

The Qurʾan offers an echo of this teaching, not a qualified endorsement.

> It may be that Allah will bring about between you and those with whom you are at enmity affection and Allah is all-powerful, and Allah is all-forgiving, all-merciful. Allah does not forbid you in regard to those who did not make war against you on account of religion and did not expel you from your homes that you deal with them with kindness and justice. Indeed Allah loves the just. Allah forbids you only in regard to those who made war against you on account of religion and expelled you from your homes and supported [others] in your expulsion, that you make friends with them and whoever makes friends with them—it is they who are the wrongdoers. (60:7-9)[13]

---

[13] Abdel Haleem's translation makes this clearer to English ears: "God may still bring about affection between you and your present enemies—God is all powerful, God is most forgiving and merciful—and He does not forbid you to deal kindly and justly with anyone who has not fought you for your faith or driven you out of your homes. God loves the just. But God forbids you to take as allies those who have fought against you for your faith, driven you out of your homes, and helped others to drive you out: any of you who take them as allies will truly be wrongdoers." *The Qurʾan*, trans. M. A. S. Abdel Haleem (Oxford, UK: Oxford University Press, 2005).

The theme is forgiveness. The Qurʾan shows there are no limits to divine forgiveness and mercy, provided there is repentance. The enemy could be defined as one who refuses to repent, perhaps because of the consequent loss of face or because they genuinely believe themselves to be in the right.

Jesus' words include no such qualification. Heartfelt mutual forgiveness is to be unconditional. In another place, Jesus answered Peter's question: "'Lord, if another member of the church sins against me, how often should I forgive? As many as seven times?' Jesus said to him, 'Not seven times, but, I tell you, seventy-seven times'" (Matt 18:21-22).[14] Forgiveness removes boundaries. There is nothing one could do that the other will not forgive.

The famous hymn to love in the First Letter of St. Paul to the Corinthians is a text Muslims would surely endorse, especially his description of the qualities of love: "Love is patient; love is kind; love is not envious or boastful or arrogant or rude. It does not insist on its own way; it is not irritable or resentful; it does not rejoice in wrongdoing, but rejoices in the truth. It bears all things, believes all things, hopes all things, endures all things" (13:4-7).

Two Insights from Later Spiritual Writers, Muslim and Christian

The challenge does not end with the inspired Scriptures. Spiritual writers in both traditions have helped to fill out the teachings on friendship.

Muḥammad ibn ʿAlī al-Bāqir (676–733 CE), the fifth Imam, said that "God will reward any man who loves another man for the sake of God, even if God knows that the second man is going to be one of the residents of Hell."[15] This teaching is even more explicit in the words of God's Prophet, "I swear by the One who

---

[14] See also Luke 17:4.

[15] Hassan ibn Fazl ibn Hassan Tabarsi, *The Lamp Niche for the Best Traditions* (Qum, Iran: Ansariyan Publications, 2007), no. 612.

controls my life that you will not enter Heaven unless you have faith. You will not have faith unless you love each other. Do you want me to tell you what to do to love each other? Just greet each other." [16]

Imam Baqir also heard from the Prophet that God said, "The most delightful friend of Mine is one who is poor and has a simple life. He best performs his worshipping in private. He is known by the people, and is content with the minimum daily bread. He does not leave much inheritance behind, and only a few will cry over his death." [17] The sixth Imam, Ja'far ibn Mu-hammad al-Sādiq (702–765 CE) offers this advice: "Fear God, and be good brothers for each other. Love each other for the sake of God, and be united. Visit each other, talk about our friendship and revive it." [18]

The mystical tradition of Christianity, as represented by St. John of the Cross, offers another emphasis. He writes, "Take God for your bridegroom and friend, and walk with him continually; and you will not sin and will learn to love, and the things you must do will work out prosperously for you." [19]

At heart is a need for detachment from worldly things: "They who are well guided from the outset do not become attached to visible instruments or burden themselves with them. They do not care to know any more than is necessary to accomplish good works because their eyes are fixed only on God, on being his friend and pleasing him; this is what they long for." [20]

The closer the intimacy with God, the clearer are the priorities in friendship: "In this interior union God communicates himself to the soul with such genuine love that neither the affection of

[16] Ibid., no. 621.

[17] Ibid., no. 1215.

[18] Ibid., no. 1025.

[19] From "Sayings of Light and Love," in *The Collected Works of St. John of the Cross*, trans. Kieran Kavanaugh and Otilio Rodriguez (Washington, DC: Institute of Carmelite Studies, 1991).

[20] *Collected Works of St. John of the Cross*, 1.3.2, p. 366.

a mother, with which she so tenderly caresses her child, nor a brother's love, nor any friendship is comparable to it." [21]

This can be taken still further. John of the Cross speaks of God as "prisoner" of the soul. "Happy is the loving soul, since she possesses God for her prisoner, and he is surrendered to all her desires. God is such that those who act with love and friendship toward him will make him do all their desire." [22]

In this intimacy the soul can look to death as "friend": "The soul thinks of death as her friend and bridegroom, and at the thought of it she rejoices as she would over the thought of her betrothed and marriage, and she longs for the day and the hour of her death more than earthly kings long for kingdoms and principalities." [23]

Some Concluding Remarks

The primary purpose of this essay is to show how the Bible speaks of friends and friendship. I have also tried to provide some examples of similarities and differences with the Qurʾanic treatment of this topic. The fundamental point of similarity is that friendship for Muslim and Christian is an enhanced relationship because it is created under the eye of a loving God. There are different models of achieving and maintaining friendship, but they overlap in the remembrance of God, a theme that underscores a core truth: God is present in the heart of each human being. But there is no treatise on friendship in either the Bible or the Qurʾan. Both Scriptures speak of the danger of associating with those who deny or desecrate the Faith. On the other hand, holy people are enriched when supported by men and women of like-minded faith who are able to share insights with them. Each also has the obligation to demonstrate in friendly relationships that human love is transformed by the

[21] Ibid., 27.1, p. 580.
[22] Ibid., 32.1, p. 599.
[23] Ibid., 11.10, p. 513.

committed intimacy each has with his or her respective Word of God into a love which enables each to aspire to the title "Friend of God."

The difference expressed in the clear command of Jesus to "love your enemies" is not as great as it sounds. Each can and should love all who live, as well as the whole of creation. The freedom that each has in responding may make such an act of love ineffective when it involves meeting the enemy. It takes two to create friendship.

Friendship in the Qur'an

Mohammad Ali Shomali

The topic of human relationships receives a great amount of attention in the Qur'an, whether it be in a positive and sympathetic way or in a negative and hostile way. Human beings need to be aware of both their friends and their enemies in order to learn how to engage with each group, how to make additional friends and defend themselves from harm caused by enemies, and, if at all possible, turn enemies into friends. There are several concepts used in the Qur'an to refer to the general notion of friendship—in other words, to a relationship that is positive, constructive, and sympathetic. Starting with an analysis of the concept of spouse (*zawj*) and then focusing on five concepts (*sāhib*, *khalil*, *akh*, *sadiq*, and *wali*) that are used in the Qur'an to refer to friendship, I will try to explore their distinctive features as well as their similarities.

Different Types of Positive Human Relationships

Studying the Qur'anic verses about different types of relationships that human beings may have with one another, we see that there are at least five concepts that the Qur'an uses in order to refer to positive, constructive, sympathetic, and supportive relationships that people can make with each other. Some of them may also be found among nonhumans, but most of them are exclusive to human beings.

Spouse

Having a spouse or a mate is one of the sympathetic, supportive, constructive, and positive relationships that human beings may have with one another, but this kind of relationship can be found among nonhumans as well. In several places, the Qur'an refers to the fact that God has made everything in pairs. Of course, there is a discussion among Qur'anic exegetes about whether "everything" really means *everything,* or whether it is only meant to refer to human beings, animals, and other living beings. Some exegetes, pointing to the duality that exists inside each atom, believe that absolutely everything is created in pairs.[1] What matters most here is that when it comes to human beings, God says that this relationship is not limited to the biological dimension of being. In plants, for example, this pairing may be only for biological reasons. In animals it may also be, at least to some extent, to provide for security and comfort. However, when it comes to human beings, the spiritual dimension precedes. According to the Qur'an, the reason God has created for us a spouse from our very own nature is so that we may be able to achieve serenity and tranquility. For example, in several places the Qur'an says that God has created spouses for us, from ourselves, so that we can find comfort and tranquility:

> And of His signs is that He created for you spouses from your own selves that you may take comfort in them, and He ordained affection and mercy between you. There are indeed signs in that for a people who reflect. (30:21)

Or in another place: "It is He who created you from a single soul, and made from it its spouses, that he might find comfort with her" (7:189).

---

[1] See, e.g., *Tafsir-e Nemuneh,* vol. 18, pp. 377–78 and vol. 22, p. 376.

Therefore, this tranquility is the outcome of a union that is partly established by God's creative act and partly by God's legislative act. In God's creation and legislation, this union is very much taken into account. God has realized all the necessary arrangements so that this union can be strong. According to the teachings of Prophet Muhammad, marriage is the most sacred construction that human beings can build,[2] and its destruction by divorce is the permissible act that is most disliked in the sight of God.[3]

The Qurʾan also extends the significance of marriage to heaven, whether it be the heaven of Adam and Eve or eternal heaven. Before entering heaven, God told Adam,

> We said, "O Adam, dwell with your spouse in paradise, and eat thereof freely whencesoever you wish; but do not approach this tree, lest you should be among the wrongdoers." (2:35)

> [Then He said to Adam,] "O Adam, dwell with your mate in paradise, and eat thereof whence you wish; but do not approach this tree, lest you should be among the wrongdoers." (7:19)

When God wanted to warn Adam about the deceptions of Satan, He told him that Satan is their enemy and he may do something in order to send both Adam and his wife outside heaven, where they would then suffer and have a miserable life:

> We said, "O Adam! This is indeed an enemy of yours and your mate's. So do not let him expel you from paradise, or you will be miserable." (20:117)

Although Adam was addressed (*Yā Adam*), the message was that Satan is your and your wife's enemy (*laka wa lizawjik*); Satan must not be allowed to cause both of you to be expelled (*lā yukhirjanna-kumā*) from heaven, or you [Adam] will be miserable (*tashqā*). I think these shifts between singular and dual pronouns

---

[2] *Bihar al-Anwar*, vol. 100, p. 222.
[3] *Al-Kafi*, vol. 5, p. 328.

show the great unity that exists between a husband and wife. In any case, Adam and Eve entered heaven together and were warned not to do anything that would lead to their being expelled together from heaven.[4] Unfortunately, they both made a grave mistake and were both asked to leave heaven.

The situation mentioned above was about a temporary heaven for Adam and Eve. However, in several places the Qur³an also refers to the existence of this type of relationship in the eternal heaven and enumerates having pure spouses as one of the greatest blessings for the people of heaven. Pious women would have pure husbands and pious men would have pure wives. The Qur³an says,

> And give good news to those who have faith and do righteous deeds, that for them shall be gardens with streams running in them: whenever they are provided with its fruit for nourishment, they will say, "This is what we were provided before," and they were given something resembling it. In it there will be chaste mates for them, and they will remain in it [forever]. (2:25)

> Say, "Shall I inform you of something better than that? For those who are Godwary there will be gardens near their Lord, with streams running in them, to remain in them [forever], and chaste mates, and God's pleasure." And God sees best the servants. (3:15)[5]

Interestingly, the Qur³an informs us that the angels who bear the Divine Throne, and those around it, pray for the believers. One of the things they continuously ask for is that God let them enter heaven along with their spouses:

> Those who bear the Throne, and those around it, celebrate the praise of their Lord and have faith in Him, and they plead for

---

[4] There is not even the slightest mention of the possibility of one spouse remaining in heaven and the other going outside. Both go to heaven or both leave heaven together.

[5] See also 4:57; 13:23.

forgiveness for the faithful: "Our Lord! You comprehend all things in mercy and knowledge. So forgive those who repent and follow Your way and save them from the punishment of hell. Our Lord! Admit them into the Gardens of Eden, which You have promised them, along with whoever is righteous among their forebears, their spouses and their descendants. Indeed You are the All-mighty, the All-wise." (40:7-8)

Thus, there seems to be no doubt about marriage being a very intimate type of positive relationship or, one might say, a very strong kind of friendship.

Friend

There are some types of relationships that seem to be exclusive to human beings and do not exist among animals. These relationships are not the same as the pairs found among other beings or even in marital relationships. There are some types of relationships which indeed demonstrate our humanity and take form when we voluntarily decide to build an intimate relationship with someone else. We may decide to become friends with a person who does not speak our language, who does not have the same ethnic background that we have, who may not even share our faith. However, we can still decide to be friends with them. We can even choose to be friends with someone who has harmed us, something that is also exclusive to human beings. God has given us the ability to look beyond all these differences and decide to be very close to one another. In the Qur'an, we find that there is no limit or restriction regarding this type of relationship as far as God is concerned. For example, the Qur'an says,

God does not forbid you in regard to those who did not make war against you on account of religion and did not expel you from your homes, that you deal with them with kindness and justice. Indeed God loves the just. God forbids you only in regard to those who made war against you on account of religion and expelled you from your homes and supported [others] in your expulsion, that you make friends with them, and whoever makes friends with them—it is they who are the wrongdoers. (60:8-9)

God does not ask us to refrain from befriending even those pagans who do not share faith in God and Islam with us on condition that they have not sent us into exile and have not fought with us to kill us. We can be good friends with them; indeed, not just friends—we can also do good to them, be kind and just with them, and provide them with what they need. According to the Qur²an, justice is something that has to be observed all the time, even with respect to our enemies. The Qur²an says,

> O you who have faith! Be maintainers, as witnesses for the sake of God, of justice, and ill feeling for a people should never lead you to be unfair. Be fair; that is nearer to Godwariness, and be wary of God. God is indeed well aware of what you do. (5:8)

So we have two main principles here: first, to be just to everyone, including those who are hostile to us; and then, to befriend and deal kindly with everyone who does not expel or kill us, including those who believe in other faiths or are faithless.

Can friendship survive death? According to the Qur²an, true friendship can survive death and continue to exist in the hereafter. In other words, true friendship is not something worldly like having money, property, position, or reputation, which would end on leaving this world. For example, if someone has a position in this world as a director, president, or king, then this position is not going to continue after they die. However, according to the Qur²an, friendship can survive death. Of course, this does not refer to all types of friendship. If friendship is based on piety, good will, and love for God, then it can continue and never ends. However, those types of friendships would cease that are based on worldly considerations or self-interest, where the parties involved in the friendship merely want to gain something for themselves and try to use the other party as a means to an end. The Qur²an says,

> O you who have faith! Spend out of what We have provided you before there comes a day on which there will be no bargaining, neither friendship, nor intercession. And the faithless—they are the wrongdoers. (2:254)

> Tell My servants who have faith to maintain the prayer and to
> spend out of what We have provided them with, secretly and
> openly, before there comes a day on which there will be neither
> any bargaining nor friendship. (14:31)

Indeed, the Qurʾan informs us that such friends will wish they
had never become friends:

> A day when the wrongdoer will bite his hands, saying, "I wish
> I had followed the Apostle's way! Woe to me! I wish I had not
> taken so and so as friend! Certainly He led me astray from the
> Reminder after it had come to me, and Satan is a deserter of
> man." (25:27-29)

The Qurʾan also tells us that such types of friendship would turn
into enmity:

> On that day, friends will be one another's enemies, except for
> the Godwary. [They will be told,] "O My servants! Today you
> will have no fear, nor will you grieve." (43:67-68)

This verse confirms that pious people will continue to remain
friends. This is so because their friendship was genuine. They
really wanted the best for the other party and, of course, because
their friendship was motivated by love for God and for good.
This type of friendship will continue up to the Day of Judgment,
and indeed afterward in heaven where it will be perfected. The
Qurʾan says,

> We will remove whatever rancour there is in their breasts, and
> streams will run for them. They will say, "All praise belongs to
> God, who guided us to this. We would have never been guided
> had not God guided us. Our Lord's apostles had certainly
> brought the truth." And the call would be made to them: "This
> is paradise, which you have been given to inherit because of
> what you used to do!" (7:43)
>   We will remove whatever rancour there is in their breasts;
> [intimate, like] brothers, [they will be reclining] on couches,
> facing one another. (15:47)

Different Terms Used for Friendship in the Qur'an

The Qur'an uses various different terms to refer to friendship:
Sāhib (plural form: *ashāb*): This term is used in different senses, but essentially it refers to something that accompanies something else, whether it be a human being or an animal,[6] a place or a time.[7] Therefore, *sāhib* is more general than friendship and just requires being together for a considerable period of time. In what follows, we will refer to some of the cases in which this term is used in the Qur'an to refer to the relationship between two people. As we will see, it is more general than friendship and is mainly used to refer to acquaintance and being together. This is why even Prophet Muhammad is introduced to the pagans who had rejected Islam as their *sahib* or companion, since they had lived with him in Mecca and knew him very well. These are the verses in which this term or its cognates are used:

> Say, "Shall we invoke besides God that which can neither benefit us nor harm us, and turn back on our heels after God has guided us, like someone seduced by the devils and bewildered on the earth, who has *companions* that invite him to guidance, [saying,] 'Come to us!'?" Say, "Indeed it is the guidance of God which is [true] guidance and we have been commanded to submit to the Lord of all the worlds." (6:71)

> Have they not reflected that there is no madness in their *companion*, [and that] he is just a manifest warner? (7:184)

> If you do not help him, then God has already helped him when the faithless expelled him, as one of two [refugees], when the two of them were in the cave, he said to his *companion*, "Do not grieve; God is indeed with us." (9:40).

> O my prison *mates*! Are different masters better, or God, the One, the All-paramount? (12:39)

---

[6] "So submit patiently to the judgment of your Lord, and do not be like the Man of the Fish who called out as he choked with grief" (68:48).

[7] Rāghib Isfahāni, *Al-Mufradāt fi Gharib al-Qur'an*, p. 475.

The guilty one will wish he could ransom himself from the punishment of that day at the price of his children, his *spouse* and his brother, his kin which had sheltered him and all those who are upon the earth, if that might deliver him. (70:11-14)

—the day when a man will evade his brother, his mother and his father, his *spouse* and his sons— that day each of them will have a task to keep him preoccupied. (80:34-37)

Khalil (plural form: *akhillā*):[8] *Khalil* means "intimate friend"[9] and the root *khullah* means affection with ultimate purity and friendship that has penetrated the heart and has gone deep into it.[10] About this type of friendship the Qurʾan says that on the Day of Judgment there will be people who will regret becoming intimate friends, *khullah*, with bad people who made them forget God and His message rather than having befriended good people (25:27-28). However, when they realize they have adopted their real enemies as friends and their real friends as enemies, their regret will be too late to change their situation.

It is interesting that even God chooses some people as His *khalil*. One can be a *khalil* of God but not a brother of God. With respect to Prophet Abraham, the Qurʾan says, "Who is better in his faith than the person who submits his will to God, being virtuous, and follows the creed of Abraham . . . and God took Abraham as a dedicated friend" (4:125).

God chose Abraham as His friend, which is a great honor for Abraham and also a great honor for all of us because we are all followers of Abraham. There are many hadiths explaining why God chose Abraham as His friend. For example, Imam Sadiq is quoted as saying, "God chose him as His friend because Abraham never rejected anyone's request and he himself never asked anyone other than God."[11]

---

[8] See 4:125; 17:73; 25:28; and 43:67.

[9] See, e.g., Turayhi, Fakhr al-Din, *Majmaʿ al-Bahrayn*, vol. 5, p. 364.

[10] Turayhi, Fakhr al-Din, *Majmaʿ al-Bahrayn*, vol. 5, p. 364.

[11] Bahrani, Sayyid Hashim, *Al-Burhān*, vol. 2, p. 177.

Sadiq (plural form: *asdiqā*): Derived from the root *sidq*, which means truth, *Sadiq* is used to refer to a friend who is honest and sincere.[12] The Qur²an uses this term in the following verses and in both cases it is used in the singular form: "Now we have no intercessors, nor do we have any sympathetic *friend*. Had there been another turn for us, we would be among the faithful" (26:100-102).[13]

Akh (plural form: *ikhwah*): Literally meaning "brother," in Arabic this term is sometimes used with other meanings. For example, in the Qur²an it is used several times in the sense of friend. Indeed, this is an extension of the literal meaning—a brother who shares the same parent(s)—to include an associate who shares the same tribe, nation, faith or ideas about life.[14] The Qur²an says, "And to [the people of] 'ād, Hud, their *brother*, He said, 'O my people, worship God! You have no other god besides Him. Will you not then be wary [of Him]?'" (7:65).

In this verse and similar verses,[15] "brother" refers to a person who is from the same nation as someone, who is very well known to them and who cares for them. In some verses, "brother" is used to refer to fellow faithful people whose relationships with each other will continue until they enter heaven together and indeed will be perfected there. For example, the Qur²an says,

> Yet if they repent and maintain the prayer and give the zakat, then they are your *brethren* in faith. We elaborate the signs for a people who have knowledge. (9:11)

> Indeed the Godwary will be amid gardens and springs. "Enter it in peace and safety!" We will remove whatever rancour there is in their breasts; [intimate like] *brothers*, [they will be reclining]

---

[12] *Lisāl al-ʿArab*, vol. 10, p. 194.

[13] See also 26:101.

[14] See e.g., Turayhi, Fakhr al-Din, *Majmaʿ al-Bahrayn*, vol. 1, p. 2; Ibn Manzur, *Lisān al-'Arab*, vol. 14, p. 1; Rāghib Isfahāni, *Al-Mufradāt fi Gharib al-Qur²an*, p. 6.

[15] See also 7:73; 7:85; 11:50, 61-84; 27:45; 29:36; 46:21.

on couches, facing one another. Therein neither weariness shall
touch them, nor will they [ever] be expelled from it. (15:45-48)

And [also for] those who came in after them, who say, "Our Lord,
forgive us and our *brethren* who were our forerunners in the faith,
and do not put any rancour in our hearts toward the faithful. Our
Lord, You are indeed most kind and merciful." (59:10)[16]

Interestingly, the Qurʾan refers to this brotherhood as a great
gift from God for the believers. The Qurʾan says,

Hold fast, all together, to God's cord, and do not be divided
[into sects]. And remember God's blessing upon you when you
were enemies, then He brought your hearts together, so you
became *brothers* with His blessing. And you were on the brink
of a pit of Fire, whereat He saved you from it. Thus does God
clarify His signs for you so that you may be guided. (3:103)

God brought together the hearts of people who used to fight
and kill each other and made them brothers; thus the people of
Mecca, the people of Medina and then all believers were made
brothers of one another. Here "brothers" is used in contrast to
"*Aʿdāʾ*" (enemies).

Akh is also used to refer to the association of bad people with
one another. The Qurʾan says, "Indeed the wasteful are *brothers*
of satans and Satan is ungrateful to his Lord" (17:27) and "Have
you not regarded the hypocrites who say to their *brethren*, the
faithless . . ." (59:11).[17]

Reflecting on these verses about brotherhood, we understand
that when it is used for nonbiological brothers, it refers either
to the members of the same nation whose lives are somehow
interconnected, such as prophets and their entire nations—including both believers and unbelievers—or to people who share
the same ideology in life, either by being believers in God or as
followers of Satan. Thus, it seems that it is not used simply for

[16] See also 33:5; 49:10-12.
[17] See also 3:156; 7:202.

two people who become each other's friends. Rather, it is used for members of the same nation, party, or camp.

Hamim: *Hamim* is sometimes used as an adjective and is normally translated as "sympathetic" or "intimate." There are two places in the Qur'an where such usage can be found:

> And no one led us astray except the guilty. Now we have no intercessors, nor do we have any *sympathetic* (or *intimate*) friend. (26:99-101)

> Good and evil [conduct] are not equal. Repel [evil] with what is best. [If you do so,] behold, he between whom and you was enmity, will be as though he were a *sympathetic* (or *intimate*) friend. (41:34)

Hamim is also sometimes used by itself as a noun and is often translated simply as friend or as a friend who is intimate, loyal, or caring. In the following verses, such usage can be found:

> Warn them of the Imminent Day when hearts will be at the throats, choking with suppressed agony, [and] the wrongdoers will have no *friend*, nor any intercessor who might be heard. (40:18)

> so he has no *friend* here today, nor any food except pus, which no one shall eat except the iniquitous. (69:35-37)

> and no *friend* will inquire about [the welfare of his] *friend*, [though they will be placed within each other's sight]. The guilty one will wish he could ransom himself from the punishment of that day at the price of his children, his spouse and his brother, his kin which had sheltered him and all those who are upon the earth, if that might deliver him. (70:10-14)

However, studying Arabic lexicons leads one to the conclusion that the literal meaning of *hamim* is a close relative or kin for whom one really cares and about whom one is concerned.[18]

---

[18] See e.g., Turayhi, Fakhr al-Din, *Majmaʿ al-Bahrayn*, vol. 6, p. 50; Ibn Manzur, *Lisān al-ʿArab*, vol. 13, p. 153; Rāghib Isfahāni, *Al-Mufradāt fi Gharib al-Qur'an*, p. 254.

When it is used as an adjective, again it is said to mean the same. For example, Raghib Isfahani interprets *hamim* in both cases as *al-qarib al-mushfiq*, which means a caring or sympathetic kin.[19]

Wali (plural form: *awliyā*).[20] *Wali* is one of the most profound concepts in Islam, especially in *Shiʿa* Islam. Briefly, in such cases, *wali* is a mutual relationship between two or more people who know each other and work for the same causes, who belong to the same party or camp and have the same leadership. Of course, their rank in that party or camp may be different. One may be the leader and another may be a follower, or both may be under another leader and so on. When it comes to pious people who are *wali* for each other, they not only know each other and work together for the same causes and under the same leadership, but they also love each other. This love between them continues even in the hereafter. This is in contrast to the bad *walis* who would become enemies and try to disassociate themselves from each other because their relationship is not based on piety, and so there is no love present. It is possible that in this world they may think they love each other, but indeed their hearts are actually divided,[21] and in the hereafter this will become obvious, so much so that the Qurʾan says that on the Day of Judgment, bad leaders will wish to distance and disassociate themselves from their followers. Disheartened by this, their followers will wish that there would be a chance for them to return to this world and distance themselves from such leaders:

> When those who were followed will disown the followers, and they will sight the punishment while all their means of recourse will be cut off, and when the followers will say, "Had there been another turn for us, we would disown them as they disown us

[19] Ibid.

[20] For example: 2:107,120,257; 3:68; 6:51.

[21] The Qurʾan says, "They will not fight against you in a body except in fortified townships or from behind walls. Their might is great among themselves. You suppose them to be a body, but their hearts are disunited." (59:14).

[now]!" Thus shall God show them their deeds as regrets for
themselves, and they shall not leave the Fire. (2:166-167)

This shows that their relationship is a very shallow one.

However, the type of relationship of *wilāya* that exists between
believers will indeed manifest itself in a stronger form in the
hereafter, where they will love and support each other forever.
One of the requirements of such a relationship between believers
is that they listen to one another and are obeyed when they
enjoin good upon one another or prohibit one another from what
is bad. No matter whether someone is, for example, an older or
a younger person, a senior or a junior scholar, rich or poor, they
have to listen to their brothers and sisters in faith who are their
awliā when they advise them correctly. The Qur'an says,

> But the faithful, men and women, are *wali* of one another: they
> bid what is right and forbid what is wrong and maintain the
> prayer, give the zakat, and obey God and His Apostle. It is they
> to whom God will soon grant His mercy. Indeed God is All-
> mighty, All-wise. (9:71)

This means that even a great scholar has to listen to a young
seminarian who gives good counsel. The scholar should not say:
"It is none of your business," or "I am more learned than you,"
and the student has a right to be obeyed. Of course, this is a
mutual relationship. Today someone may ask me to correct my-
self and tomorrow it may happen that I correct the person who
corrected me.

Therefore, when there is *wilāyah* between two people, there
must be mutual knowledge, mutual love, and mutual obedience.
It is not merely the kind of official relationship which usually
exists within companies or political parties. When one works in
an office, one is not bound to love one's boss or colleagues in
one's heart. Office workers only ask and expect one to show
respect for their fellows, and for everyone to do what they are
supposed to do. However, in the relationship of *wilāyah*, one has
to love. Everyone involved in that type of relationship is required
to love, and it is this love that then leads to obedience. We obey

because we love the one who instructs us and the values that are at stake.

Reflection on the above verses of the Qur'an leads to the conclusion that human beings can have positive and sympathetic relationships with each other in different ways and at different levels. Most of these relationships can be shared with those who are pious, who are believers in God and have good will, from across different schools of religion, especially when it comes to the followers of Abraham.

Further reflection on the above and similar verses also shows that there are two types of people who are totally different from a friend, whether that friend be *khalil, sadiq, akh, sahib, wali.* Either they are just different from us, or they are in sharp contrast to us, and it is only the latter that could be called an enemy. For example, the one who is not your *khalil* is not necessarily your enemy. We must not think that everyone who is not our friend is therefore our enemy. Interestingly enough, however, with regard to all five categories of friendship, if someone is really in conflict with us and works against us, such a one is called *ʾaduww* (enemy; the plural form is *aʿdā*).

I hope and pray that God the Almighty would guide and help all believers and all people of good will to recognize each other and to become true and lasting friends of one another so that day by day we become closer and closer.

Love and Friendship

Prerequisite and Goal of Monastic/Muslim Dialogue

Mohsen Javadi

Nasir al-Din Tusi (1201–1274), one of the leading Muslim peripatetic philosophers, proposed the following definition of love:

> The true meaning of "love" is the quest for union with that thing with which the seeker conceives its perfection to be united; and as we have said that the perfection and nobility of each existent thing is in accordance with the unity that has been effused upon it; therefore, love is the quest for nobility and virtue and perfection.[1]

The fundamental origin of love in the human world is the search for perfection. Since human beings are deficient with regard to possible perfections, but are endowed with the love of perfection in their nature, they long for everything thought of as leading to their perfection and excellence.

Tusi's definition would seem to be contrary to our intuitions about love and friendship. First, it assumes a sort of deficiency on the part of the persons engaged in love; second, it is based

---

[1] Nasir al-Din Tusi, *The Nasirean Ethics*, trans. G. M. Wickens (London: George Allen & Unwin, 1964), p. 196.

on an egoistic conception of human voluntary love and regards the issue of love in a manner that appears to be selfish.

In response to the first problem, we can limit Tusi's definition to "human voluntary love," recognizing that there are other kinds of love, such as God's love for His servants, especially for the pious and faithful. Since God is already perfect and therefore does not gain anything from His servants, God's love is not based on deficiency or a striving for perfection.

With regard to the second problem, I believe that Tusi's definition is not really egoistic. When one aims to perfect oneself, a necessary condition for achieving this aim is abandoning selfishness. Human perfection is only achieved through altruistic actions. Real self-interest and self-love, which is innate, can only be fully satisfied by sacrificing one's egoistic desires in favor of the interests of others.

Friendship

In light of the above definition of love we can say that friendship is a mutual relation of love between two or among a few persons. Someone may like many people, but his or her friends are few: "The true friend cannot be found in great numbers, for he is noble and rare, and esteem is one of the concomitants of paucity."[2]

In friendship, love is mutual; each of the two considers union with the other as a way to his or her perfection.

> Friendship is a kind of love, but it denotes something more particular than love. It is affection in its very essence and it does not take place among a large group, as is the case with love.[3]

Love is in the heart, but friendship, although rooted in the heart, is an external social phenomenon. Without love, there can be no true friendship. But love alone is not sufficient for friend-

---

[2] Ibid., 243.

[3] Ahmad Ibn Muhammad Miskawayh, *The Refinement of Character* [*Tahdhib al-Akhlaq*], trans. Constantine K. Zurayh (Beirut: American University of Beirut, 1968), p.125.

ship. Aristotle says that there are different causes of love; hence the ways of loving are different, and so are the friendships.[4]

After a detailed discussion of the requirement of proportional equality of loving in the relationship of friendship, Aristotle says that there is no friendship between human beings and gods.

> This is clear if friends come to be separated by some wide gap in virtue, vice, wealth, or something else; for then they are friends no more, and do not even expect to be. This is most evident with gods, since they have the greatest superiority in all goods.[5]

Aristotle's commentators have usually said the reason he asserts that friendship between a human being and a god is impossible is because the condition of proportional equality is lacking. They claim that this is why Aristotle placed this claim after a discussion of unequal friends. However, Aristotle does accept a kind of asymmetrical friendship between unequal partners, as in the case of the relationship between a ruler and the ruled or a father and his children. So the mere fact of inequality between humans and gods is not a sufficient reason to deny the possibility of friendship between them.

What makes such a friendship impossible can be found in Aristotle's discussion about wanting the greatest good for a friend. Aristotle explains that since friendship is based on the relation of love, which, by definition, assumes a sort of mutual need to achieve perfections, it is not possible between gods and humans, since gods have no need. According to Aristotle, gods can be beloved by people, but they cannot love those who serve them, since they are too perfect and immaculate to gain anything from their worshippers.

Contrary to Aristotle, the Abrahamic faiths allow for the possibility of love between unequals, even when there is nothing to be gained and no need filled for one of the parties to the

---

[4] Aristotle, *Nicomachean Ethics*, trans. Terence Irwin, 2nd ed. (Cambridge: Hackett Publishing Company, 1999), bk. 8, chap. 7 (1158b 18–19).

[5] Ibid. (1158b 25–27).

relationship. When we come to the teachings and example of a prophet like Jesus, for instance, we see evidence of real friendship between unequal partners—between Jesus and his apostles, as well as between Jesus and ordinary people.

The love of God for his creatures in general, and his friendship with select individuals, such as his prophets, in particular, is a cornerstone of Islamic teachings regarding the way we are to live. Although there is an unconceivable superiority on the one side and inferiority and lack of perfection on the other, nevertheless, the strongest kind of friendship can exist between God and human beings.

Allah's love of his creatures is the best context in which a friendly relation with him may be achieved. However, we need to respond to the love of God appropriately in order to make possible this mutual friendship between God and us. The only requirement is that we love him sincerely. Doing so leads to a long-lasting friendship which results in our felicity and salvation. In the words of the Noble Qurʾan, "O you who have faith! Should any of you desert his religion, Allah will soon bring a people whom He loves and who loves Him" (5:54). And again, "And hasten toward your Lord's forgiveness and a paradise as vast as the heavens and the earth, prepared for the Godwary—those who spend in ease and adversity, and suppress their anger, and excuse [the faults of] the people, and Allah loves the virtuous" (3:133-4).

In Islamic literature, and especially in the Noble Qurʾan, different terms are used for friendship. *Khalil* is the closest word to "friend"; it and its derivatives are used in the Qurʾan seven times. For instance, "And Allah took Abraham as a friend [*Khalil*]" (4:125). Abraham is also referred to as God's friend in the Bible: "And he was called God's friend" (James 2:23).

It is interesting to note that the prophet Muhammad said that "God took Abraham as a friend only because of his feeding of food [to others] and praying of prayers in the night while the people were asleep."[6] Feeding the poor is the symbol of all righ-

---

[6] M. M. Rayshahri, *Scale of Wisdom*, English and Arabic Edition (London: Islamic College for Advanced Studies Publications, 2008), p. 1031.

teous deeds in society; prayer in the silence of the night is the symbol of the love and remembrance of God. Taken together, they make friendship with God possible and save humanity from wretchedness.

The Importance of Friendship

Friendship has long been admired as a human value, and philosophers have talked of its importance in one way or another. Friendship has also been highlighted in religious teachings. The Qurʾan, for instance, says, " But, the faithful, men and women are comrades of one another; they bid what is right and forbid what is wrong and maintain the prayer, give the *zakāt*, and obey Allah and His Apostle" (9:71). Imam Ali says, "O, Kumayl! Say what is just in any condition. Be friends with the righteous and avoid the evil doers, stay away from the hypocrites and do not accompany the treacherous."[7]

Having proposed "religious brotherhood" as an expression of friendship, the Qurʾan was responsible for a new development in the primitive Arab society, which, prior to Muhammad, did not recognized "friendship" outside the bond of family or tribe. One of the outcomes of Islam in Arab society was the creation of affection and brotherhood[8] among the Arabs. God says, "And remember Allah's blessing upon you when you were enemies, then He brought your hearts together, so you became brothers with Allah's blessing" (3:103).

Love for Allah

The concept of "love for Allah"—meaning "love for the sake of Allah"—is present in many Islamic traditions and is regarded

---

[7] Hussain Noori, *Mustadrak-ul-Wasaʾil* vol. 12 (Lebanon: Muʾasasat Al al-Bay li Ihya al-Turath, 1408 AH [1987]), p. 197.

[8] This means a deep form of friendship. In religious texts, this usually refers to the equality of human beings as servants of God.

as one of the main essentials of faith. Managing one's love on the basis of love for Allah will guarantee one's faith and eternal salvation. One day holy Prophet Muhammad asked his companions, "What handle of faith is the firmest and most secure of all?" Everyone had an answer, but the Prophet Muhammad said, "Surely, the firmest handle of faith is love for the sake of Allah and anger for His sake." [9]

A faithful person who loves Allah will love and respect other persons who are his vicegerents or representatives on the earth. The love of the faithful for other people is not merely dependent, as Aristotle said, on social needs. Rather, it is rooted in the faithful person's love for Allah. How can a person whose heart is replete with love for Allah hate or hold a grudge against someone else? Accordingly, Islamic traditions, particularly the Shiʾite hadiths, have repeatedly suggested that living religiously is naught else but loving for the sake of Allah: "Religion is not but love in Allah."

Given the above explanations of human love and friendship, it follows that one who lacks humility will be incapable of true friendship. This is because true friendship is based on love, human love motivated by the desire to achieve perfection in recognition of the perfections in the beloved and the flaws in the self.

Love and Friendship as the Prerequisite and Goal of Dialogue

Dialogue as a social phenomenon has a long history. There are different forms of dialogue because of the differences of the participants and their ends and aims.

Dialogue among Muslims differs from that between Muslims and Christians, because in the former case there is a shared the-

---

[9] Muhammad ibn Yaʾqub ibn Ishaq alKulaini, *Al-Kafi*, vol. 3 (Teheran: Dar al-Hadith, 2012), p. 324.

ology on the basis of which different positions are debated. Between Muslims and Christians, on the other hand, there is no expectation that theological argument will lead to a change in basic beliefs. In intra-Muslim discussion, debate has the character of an insider's discussion. In interreligious dialogue, however, each party looks at the theology of the dialogue partner as distinct. There are different aims that we can achieve by dialogue between Muslims and Christians in general and among Benedictines and Shiʿa in particular. The urgency of dialogue for the believers of different Abrahamic religions comes not from the need to gain better understanding of each other's faith, but from the need to find a broad, deep way of cooperating in the struggle against the atheism of the modern world.

Shahid Mutahhari contrasts doxastic atheism with another form of atheism that he calls moral materialism. Doxastic atheism is the denial of a supernatural world in general and the denial of God in particular. According to these atheists, human life is purely physical and ends with death. The only rationale for some superficially altruistic behavior is a hidden but deliberate egoism. Moral materialism does not deny God or supernatural realms, but it prompts us to live as though there is no God, no spirit, and no afterlife. Moral materialism mean believing like real believers but behaving like nonbelievers. The changes that occur in the soul as a result of habitual bad behavior and sin can result in a change in one's theoretical outlook in such a way that eventually one openly denies religious truths.[10] In the words of the Qurʾan, "Then the face of those who committed misdeeds was that they denied the signs of Allah and they used to deride them" (30:10).

Although many religious scholars think that the most dangerous form of atheism is doxastic, there are good reasons to believe that moral materialism is more dangerous and more persistent than doxastic atheism. First, one who considers himself to be a

---

[10] Morteza Mutahhari, *The Causes of Inclination into Materialism* (Qom: Sadra, 2001), pp. 166–74.

believer will not question his own views and will not enter into the kind of dialogue that might give him reason to reform himself. Second, to change the ideas of one who is virtuous but has mistaken views is much easier than changing the behavior of one who has correct views but leads a sinful life.

The reason for dialogue, then, is to share our understanding and experiences of these common threats and to look for possible defenses against this widespread atheism. Of course, dialogue also provides us an opportunity to correct our mistaken views about one another's beliefs. In addition, there are immense practical benefits to be gained through dialogue. If we focus on the practical aims that dialogue can have and that will be of mutual benefit to our communities, we need have no fear that engaging in dialogue will weaken or challenge our faith by bringing up arguments for which we have no ready response.

Dialogue helps us to know each other better than we did before and to recognize the common values and beliefs that have been transmitted by our Abrahamic ancestors. Children of Abraham engaged in a dialogue can maintain their differences while becoming unified in the face of common problems. What is the danger of poverty for faith? How may it lead a person to practical atheism? What prompts people to seek out worldly idols to satisfy their needs that then lead them to theoretical atheism? In dialogue, we can become clearer about the dangers to faith brought by global poverty or discrimination and look for ways we can work together to overcome these evils.

The first end of dialogue is to remove whatever misconceptions we may have of each other's faith. But dialogue goes beyond this theoretical enterprise to arrive at a practical end, such as coming up with ways we can together begin to combat the causes of practical atheism, including the misuse of religion to fan the flames of sectarianism and promote civil war and conflict, often for the sake of worldly gain.

Dialogue is related to love and friendship in two ways. First, there is a type of friendship that is needed before dialogue begins. This friendship is a condition that is necessary for true dialogue, and without it, the exchange will never rise above the level of debate. This friendship is one in which the parties to dialogue are ready to listen to one another, to expose their strengths and weaknesses, to search together for truth and understanding, and to engage in a common practice.

The second kind of friendship is one that comes into being as a result of dialogue. Once we discover the perfections in the characters of our dialogue partners, and the truths that are made evident to us in the course of dialogue—truths we otherwise would have neglected—we can seek to learn from our partners and share, to some extent, in these perfections and in the discovered truths. This is another form of friendship—one in which we assist one another in the acquisition of virtue as a result of dialogue. It is this kind of deepened friendship that can form a basis for cooperation in meeting contemporary challenges to religious life in a world dominated by practical materialism and shallow hedonism.

A Monastic Approach
to Friendship between Religions

Benoît Standaert

It is a good thing to speak together about friendship. Conversation about friendship is itself a source of friendship. It nourishes friendly relations, purifies them, elevates them, and opens them to new and ever wider horizons.

As a Benedictine monk I belong to a tradition that has cultivated friendship from its earliest years (fourth century CE). During my first years in the monastery, monastic literature introduced me to friendship as a literary theme and a social reality. Later, philosophical studies offered me an opportunity to reflect more deeply on this subject. I have always been eager to take notes on this theme in the hope of one day publishing something about it. Today I am happy to be invited to reflect about friendship in the new context of an interreligious encounter.

We may consider the theme in the image of a tree. I will first speak about the roots of friendship, then its trunk, and finally, the many branches that have appeared over the centuries.

The Roots: Ancient Greek and Roman Philosophy

The first thing to be noted is that the theme of friendship has been central in the philosophical tradition of the West, going all the way back to Pythagoras and the Seven Sages, as well as to Plato and Aristotle. It continues to be present throughout the Hellenistic period, in both philosophical and religious circles, whether of the Stoics or the Epicureans, the Jews or the Christians. The theme is still present in contemporary philosophical literature, for example, in the writings of the French-Jewish philosopher Jacques Derrida.

Ancient authors expressed the meaning of friendship in many beautiful maxims, and it may be fitting to remember some of them briefly:

> Friends have all things in common [*tois philois ta panta koina.*] (*Koinônia* was central in friendship; it meant the sharing together of all goods).
>
> There is no friendship except between equals.
>
> To like and dislike the same things, that is indeed true friendship. [*idem velle, idem nolle . . .*]
>
> A friend is another self.
>
> A true friend is one soul in two bodies.
>
> My friend is the other half of my soul.
>
> Friends are one soul and one heart.
>
> Without virtue, friendship cannot exist at all.

The conviction of ancient philosophers that friendship is worth more than anything else was expressed in such maxims as

> Without friends no one would be able to bear the burden of life, even if he possessed all the other goods of the world.
>
> True friendship has a beginning but no end.
>
> One only becomes a friend after having been tested.
>
> One is friend for life and in death. (The blood pact between friends was a very frequent practice among the ancient Dorians; it meant that the only thing that could separate friends was death).

Only virtuous people who together choose what is most noble
can worthily be called friends. (Brigands and thieves come together to achieve a common goal, but they are a gang, not a
circle of friends.)

Finally, let us quote the famous definition of friendship given
by Cicero: "For friendship is nothing else than an accord in all
things, divine and human, conjoined with mutual goodwill and
affection [*caritate*], and I am inclined to think that, with the exception of wisdom, no better thing has been given to man by the
immortal gods" (106–143).[1] This definition comes very close to
the one he gives elsewhere of wisdom: "Wisdom is an acquaintance with all divine and human affairs, and a knowledge of the
cause of everything."[2]

There is a double trajectory within this wide tradition. For
some, the number of friends one has can only be a happy few,
or even only one. Thus, if a person claims to have many friends,
he or she in fact has none. For the great authors on the topic of
friendship, it is the result of a careful, discerning choice, the fruit
of an election.

For others, on the contrary, friendship is a political virtue that
is at the very heart of society. We pursue this virtue together, and
by so doing build up a city and a society marked by the highest
degree of humanity. In this tradition everyone is a potential friend,
even the one who may appear at first glance to be an enemy.

So much for the roots. Let us now consider the trunk.

The Trunk: Philosophical Schools
and the First Christian Community

This type of friendship, ever more precisely defined by the
masters of the Hellenistic period, will influence all philosophical

---

[1] Marcus Tullius Cicero, *Laelius de amicitia*, trans. W. A. Falconer, bk. 154,
vol. 20, Loeb Classical Library (New York: Putnam and Sons, 1923).

[2] Marcus Tullius Cicero, *Tusculan Disputations*, trans. J. E. King, bk. 141, vol.
18, Loeb Classical Library (New York: Putnam and Sons, 1923), pp. v, 3, 7.

and religious communities. In ancient Judaism we see the formation of groups called *chavuroth* (*chaver* is a friend). In his work
on the contemplative life, *De vita contemplativa,* Philo of Alexandria (20 BCE–50 CE) refers to such a society, the *Therapeutae.*
Another such group within ancient Judaism was the Essenes,
who were described by Flavius Josephus in his work *The Jewish
War* (II, 8), and whose existence was confirmed by some of the
texts discovered in Qumran.

The community of the first Christians in Jerusalem also adopted
several principles and practices of the great philosophical tradition
of friendship as transmitted by Pythagoras, Plato, and Aristotle.
Luke, the author of the Acts of the Apostles, is clearly trying to
show the superiority of the Christian faith when he reminds his
readers that what the philosophers proposed as ideal—namely,
the common ownership of goods, which are then shared according to the need of each—is what the Christian community prac-
ticed from the very beginning (see Acts 2:42,44; 4,32).

Luke is not the only New Testament author who emphasizes
this ideal. According to the Evangelist John, on the night before
he died, Jesus said, "No one has greater love than this, to lay
down one's life for one's friends" (John 15:13). Paul recalled one
of the philosophical maxims on friendship in order to stress that
God in Christ has shown us a much greater love than that spoken
of by the philosophers: "Indeed, rarely will anyone die for a
righteous person—though perhaps for a good person someone
might actually dare to die. But God proves his love for us in that
while we still were sinners Christ died for us" (Rom 5:7-8).

We may say, in conclusion, that friendship, one of the highest
cultural values of pre-Christian antiquity, was successfully in-
tegrated into the faith and practice of the followers of Jesus from
the very beginning of the Christian movement.

The Branches of the Tree: Monks and Friendship

This theme of friendship will be developed over the succeed-
ing centuries, especially in the monastic tradition. Since I have

been asked to reflect on the monastic understanding and practice of friendship, let me expand on this dimension for a bit before trying to see what friendship may mean for those who engage in an interreligious dialogue.

With regard to the revival of the philosophical theme of friendship in the Christian monastic milieu, we can make four observations. First, over the centuries monastic literature continuously and explicitly takes up the theme of friendship as developed by the ancient authors. From beginning to end, the letters of Saint Basil the Great (329–379) evoke the ideal of friendship known to the Greeks. The sharing inherent in community life—the famous *koinonia*—is one of the favorite topics of his correspondence. Saint Augustine (354–430), who was a monk before becoming a baptized Christian, was introduced to the ideal of friendship through his early formation in the Pythagorean milieu that he became familiar with in Italy. Saint Ambrose (330–397), his master, borrowed largely from the writings of the Stoics, especially from the *De officiis* of Cicero. When in the eleventh and twelfth centuries there was a renaissance of that philosophy within the Cistercian movement, we find Aelred of Rievaulx (1110–1167) explicitly quoting Cicero's *De amicitia*, and William of Saint-Thierry (c. 1075–1148), constantly referring to the *Letters* of Seneca to Lucilius. Aelred reformulates the evolution of friendship in perfect consonance with the Ancients when we writes, "Friendship is born between good people, develops within the best, but is fulfilled only between those who are perfect."[3]

Second, in their treatises on the topic of friendship, monastic Church Fathers of the third, fourth, and fifth centuries enriched what they received from the Ancients by referring to the Bible, especially to passages from the First Testament. The friendship between David and Jonathan is frequently mentioned. There are also many good examples in the sixteenth Conference, *On Friend-*

---

[3] *Spiritual Friendship*, bk. 2, p. 15. *Inter bonos oriri potest, inter meliores proficere ; consummari autem inter perfectos.*

ship, of John Cassian (c. 360–435) and in Saint Augustine's rule for monastic men and women, in which he rephrases the principles of the Pythagorean School in biblical terms. Another example is the commentary of Evagrius Ponticus (345–399) on the book of Proverbs, where he writes,

> If friendship makes free (see Proverbs), if truth makes free (see John), if the Lord makes free (see Paul), then "truth" and "friendship" are Christ. That is why those who possess the knowledge [*gnosis*] of Christ are friends of one another. This is the reason the Savior called his disciples friends and John [the Baptist] was "the friend of the Bridegroom," as were Moses and all the saints. It is only in that kind of friendship that the friends of the same person are also the friends of one another.[4]

Third, there was also some variance in the way friendship was presented by early Christian writers. For the Ancients, friendship was unthinkable between persons who were not of the same social class. You had to be "equal" to know friendship. Christianity, however, proposed that true reciprocity is possible even between persons who are not of equal social standing, intellectual ability, gender, or state of life (monk, bishop, married lay person). By writing letters—one of the privileged ways of developing friendship in every age—sisters and brothers could experience reciprocity and real friendship, even if direct social contact was formally not allowed and physically often impossible.

Fourth, several new accents were also added when Christians reflected on friendship. One of them is "Friendship in the Trinitarian God." Richard of Saint-Victor (+ 1173) meditates on the perfection of charity which he contemplates in God himself. At the end of a long argument in which he traces the interpersonal experience of charity-friendship back to the inner exchange between the Father, the Son, and the Holy Spirit, he concludes, "The perfection of charity requires a Trinity of persons, without

---

[4] *Scholia* 304, on Prov 25:10a, *Sources Chrétiennes*, 340, p. 397. See John 8:31-32; Gal 3:13; John 3:29; 15:15; Exod 33:11; Jas 2:23.

which charity cannot exist in its fullness. Thus, total and full perfection does not exist without perfect charity and certainly not without the true Trinity. There is therefore not only plurality but true trinity in the true Unity and true unity in the true Trinity."[5]

Another accent is "Friendship in Christ." As we have already seen, Evagrius says in his interpretation of Scripture that "truth" and "friendship" indicate Christ himself who liberates us. Augustine ends his monastic rule with the impressive image of the community of brothers (and the community of sisters) united around Christ, who is divine Wisdom and Beauty standing in their midst.[6] "Philocalia" and "Philosophia," love of Beauty and love of Wisdom, make the community a circle of lovers who love one another by together loving Wisdom, who is Christ in their midst. In the *Confessions*, Augustine writes, "Friendship is not true, O Lord, if you yourself do not bind together those who are attached to you through the charity that the Holy Spirit who is given to us, pours out in our hearts." And further on, "Happy is he who loves his friend in you, O Lord, and his enemy for you."[7] Augustine's contemporary, Paulinus of Nola (c. 354–431), expresses much the same sentiment as he discovers in the other someone who is already "the image of God": "Love your God, and in your God love your friend who is the image of you, God, as he himself can, by loving God in the same way, love you in God."

Finally, Robert Grosseteste (1175–1253), the well-educated bishop of Lincoln and teacher at Oxford, reveals both his extensive knowledge of the ancient teaching regarding friendship and his own originality when we writes,

---

[5] *De Trinitate*, 3, 11.

[6] "The Lord grant that you may observe all these precepts in a spirit of charity, as lovers of spiritual beauty, and may spread abroad the sweet odor of Christ by a good life, not as slaves living under the law but as men and women living in freedom under grace." Adolar Zumkeller, *Augustine's Rule: A Commentary*, ed, John E. Rotelle, trans. Matthew J. O'Connell, chap. 8 (Villanova, PA: Augustinian Press, 1987).

[7] Augustine, *Confessions*, 4.9.14.

According to the law of friendship, each of the two friends is the alter ego of his friend, in virtue of the bond of love and unity that has been forged between them [and also in virtue of the] unity of will with regard to things that are good [a clear reference to the *Idem velle idem nolle in rebus honestis* of Sallust (*De conjuratione Catilinae*, 20,4)]. In the same way, the son is "the alter ego" of his father. When we consider this, can we not say that the unity of Christian believers with Christ is even greater than the unity of friends with one another, since, in virtue of creation, they are children of the God who became human? Can we not also say that their rebirth [through faith and baptism] reinforces their filiation, and that they are sons while sharing the nature of Christ, receiving his illumination and being all together strongly united by an indissoluble love?[8]

Yet another new accent is "Friendship in the Spirit." According to biblical revelation, God is spirit and love. In the eleventh-century dialogue on spiritual friendship already referred to, Aelred's friend Yves asks him, "Should I say of friendship what John, the friend of Jesus, said of charity, 'God is friendship'?" Aelred replies, "This is novel indeed and lacks the authority of the Scriptures. The rest of that verse about charity, however, I surely do not hesitate to attribute to friendship, because 'the one who remains in friendship remains in God, and God in him.'"[9]

"Friendship in the Church" is another new accent. Here we find a coming together of the political and the elective dimension of friendship. Jesus said, "Where two or three are gathered together in my name, I am there in the midst of them" (Matt 18:20). To be a Christian is to become one body with Christ, entering thereby into friendship with God. In the fourteenth century some circles of devout people called themselves *amici Dei*, "friends of God."

Finally, there is "Friendship beyond death." We may call this the *eschatological* dimension of friendship, and it is typical of the Christian approach. Aelred of Rievaulx ends his treatise on spiritual friendship with this beautiful vision of heaven:

[8] *Ex rerum initiatorum*, pp. 140f.
[9] Aeldred of Rievaulx, *On Spiritual Friendship*, 1, p. 70.

He looks to a future having a fullness of all beatitude, where
fear, the cause of all uneasiness and solicitude, shall be no more;
where all the adversity which we have borne for one another
shall be warded off, and even the sting of death shall have been
destroyed (cf. 1 Cor 15, 25). With security in a firm grasp, we
shall rejoice in the eternity of the highest good. Friendship,
which is of the few here, shall be transfused among all there,
and shall flow back again from all upon God, since God shall
be all things in all.[10]

A More Recent Branch:
Friendship and Interreligious Dialogue

If it is true that memory is the wellspring of the present, we
may now ask how our memory of this treasure of humanity
might apply to the relationship between religions, and specifi-
cally between Christianity and Islam. The question is huge and
may even appear too immense to be considered realistically. But
is it not so that often when we ask really big questions, we are
forced to dig more deeply than usual into our own traditions?
In this case we may hope to discover what is still hidden yet
present in our own treasures and what absolutely must be re-
trieved if we are to experience the present and future meeting
of the great religions of the world as a time of a blessing for all
humankind.

First of all, it should be noted that relations between great
entities are always mediated by individuals who establish trust
based on mutual knowledge and reciprocal esteem and sharing.
The dual nature of friendship as described by ancient Greek and
Roman authors—one more political and universal, the other
more selective—can certainly be an inspiration to persons from
different cultural and religious backgrounds. Friends are those
who accept and refuse the same things (*idem velle, idem nolle*),
who together choose the highest values of beauty and goodness,

---

[10] Aelred of Rievaulx, *On Spiritual Friendship,* 3, p. 134.

who agree deeply on divine and human matters. We all need to travel the long road of becoming familiar with and growing in love for another person if we are to be filled with esteem for what is at the heart of his or her religious faith and practice. If individuals can arrive at such mutual understanding, this will surely have an effect on the religious communities to which they belong.

However, it should be noted that the dynamics at work in interpersonal encounters are not necessarily the same for encounters between greater entities like religious or philosophical traditions. When I look at my own Christian tradition, I can become overwhelmed by the extent of the difficulties that stand in the way of mutual knowledge and esteem between Catholics, Protestants, and Orthodox. During the last century, Christians rejoiced in the development of a vibrant ecumenical movement among the major branches of the faith. But we still have a long way to go. Even within the Roman Catholic Church, the different religious orders—Jesuits, Dominicans, Franciscans, and so on—still have a long way to go to come to a positive understanding of one another. We can recall a time when there was great rivalry between "black monks" and "white monks" (Benedictines and Cistercians). Today we rejoice that we are able to sit around the same table as friends.

In this context, I remember the observation of a famous Dominican theologian, Father Yves Congar (1904–1995). With humor, insight, and humility he recalled the strange contrast between the formation for interpersonal relations he received within his own Dominican order and the totally different behavior that was allowed when it came to dealing with members of another congregation or order. Within our own community, he said, we were expected to be humble, obedient, understanding of the weaknesses of the others, full of patience and so on. But as soon as we had to defend the interests of the Dominican order against the Franciscans or the Jesuits, for instance, the rules changed and any tactic was allowed, as long as we came out on top. I mention this to show that it is not an easy step to go from the individual and personal level to the corporate level.

The phenomenon of religious rivalry seems to be universal. I was part of a group that went to Japan for a meeting with Buddhist monks (1998). We discovered that there are no less than nine different branches of Japanese Buddhism. We were the guests of two schools of the Zen Buddhist tradition, Rinzai and Soto, but even these two sub-sub-groups did not meet one another very often, and they were even less accustomed to meet members of some of the other branches of Japanese Buddhism. In fact, comments about other Buddhist groups were met with an icy reserve. Sometimes it is easier to establish a good relationship with people who are totally different from us than it is with those who are only slightly different. To give another example, how many jokes did we fashion to try to overcome the little and yet maddening differences between the Flemish and Dutch people!

There have been some great witnesses to interreligious friendship, pioneering geniuses like Mahatma Gandhi, Louis Massignon, Thomas Merton, Chiara Lubich, and Christian de Chergé and the brothers of Tibhirine in Algeria. The greatness of their testimony is that they did more than have good individual relationships with their neighbors. They tried to open a way for two or more religions to meet in friendship.

The philosopher Paul Ricoeur, in response to a question posed by the theologian Hans Küng in a public interview, said, "It is only in depth that distances are shortened." He then went on to say,

> If religions are to survive, they will have to respond to a number of different requirements. In the first place, they will have to give up all claims to power, except that of a vulnerable word. Moreover, they will have to put compassion ahead of doctrinal rigidity. Above all—and the hardest of all—they will have to look deeply into their teachings for the "over and above" that has not yet been put in words but thanks to which each one may hope to join the others.[11]

11 The televised interview (ARTE) took place on April 15, 1996. The quoted passage is found in Gabriel Ringlet, *L'Évangile d'un libre penseur* (Paris: Albin Michel, 2002), p. 220.

Christian de Chergé and an Algerian Muslim friend used the image of digging a well to describe their spiritual conversations. The water we seek, they both came to understand, does not belong to any particular religion or denomination. In silence and adoration we dig our wells in the hope of finding not Christian water or Muslim water, but God's water.

One of the teachings on friendship we received through the tradition was on the eschatological dimension of friendship. Our deepest hope is that friendship is stronger than death. Even on the other shore we shall meet as friends. The evangelist Luke, who also wrote the Acts of the Apostles, recounts the martyrdom of Stephen, who was stoned to death outside the gates of Jerusalem just a few years after the death of Jesus. As the stones were hurled at him, he prayed for his enemies, asking God that they be spared and forgiven. One of his enemies was a young man of Tarsus by the name of Saul who later became the apostle Paul (Acts 7:58-60).

Thomas More (1478–1535), who was condemned to death for opposing the divorce and remarriage of Henry VIII, addressed a word to his former friend, King Henry, expressing his hope that one day they might sit together at the same heavenly banquet.

Conflicts and differences will inevitably arise. Let each of us deal with them in such a way that we will not be excluded from the eschatological banquet table to which we are all invited, the table that the Scriptures and the fifth and last surah of the holy Qurʾan declare is already being prepared for us.

Conclusion

We have considered the roots, trunk, and branches of the long Western tradition of reflection on friendship, looking more closely at the insights offered by Christian monasticism. I recently received a book written by Brother John of Taizé, a monastic community in France that was founded in 1940 by Roger Schutz. In 2005, their founder, who was ninety years old, was stabbed to death by a mentally ill person while he, the monastic community, and about three thousand young people were praying together in church. The book emphasizes the centrality of friendship in the monastic community of Taizé and in all the writings of Brother Roger. Taizé exists to bring together in unity what is different; it is a striking example of how the ancient theory and practice of friendship are still alive in monastic communities today.

Let me finish with the words of two exceptional witnesses to the deepest meaning of friendship, Thomas More and Christian de Chergé.

As Thomas More was about to be executed, he addressed his judges, all of whom he knew personally:

> More have I not to say (my Lords) but like as the blessed Apostle St. Paul, as we read in the Acts of the Apostles, was present, and consented to the death of St. Stephen, and kept their clothes that stoned him to death, and yet be they now both twain holy saints in heaven, and shall continue there friends forever, so I verily trust and shall therefore right heartily pray, that though your Lordships have now in earth been judges to my condemnation, we may yet hereafter in heaven merrily all meet together to our everlasting salvation.[12]

Christian de Chergé, realizing that he might be a victim of the violence that was enveloping Algeria in the 1990s, wrote a last will and testament a little more than a year before his death. In it he expressed his hope for reconciliation—even with the one who might believe that by killing him he would be doing his duty:

> This is what I shall be able to do, if God wills—immerse my gaze in that of the Father, and contemplate with him his children of Islam just as he sees them, all shining with the glory of Christ, the fruit of His Passion, and filled with the Gift of the Spirit, whose secret joy will always be to establish communion and to refashion the likeness, playfully delighting in the differences.

[12] William Roper and N. Harpsfield, *Lives of Saint Thomas* (London: Dent, 1963).

This life lost, totally mine and totally theirs, I thank God who seems to have willed it entirely for the sake of that JOY in everything and in spite of everything. In this THANK YOU, which sums up my whole life to this moment, I certainly include you, friends of yesterday and today, and you, my friends of this place, along with my mother and father, my sisters and brothers and their families, the hundredfold granted as was promised!

And also you, the friend of my final moment, who would not be aware of what you were doing, Yes, I also say this THANK YOU and this A-DIEU to you, in whom I see the face of God. And may we find each other, happy good thieves in Paradise, if it pleases God, the Father of us both. AMEN! In sha'Allah!

Algiers, December 1, 1993
Tibhirine, January 1, 1994
Christian

Friend of God

Abraham and the Four Birds

Farrokh Sekaleshfar

He loves them and they will love Him. (5:54)

Whoever I [God] love, I shall kill. (Sacred Tradition)

When attempting to define the term "friendship," Ibn ʿArabi (d. 1240AH), the celebrated Shiʿa Gnostic, writes,

> People are at variance as to the definition of *muḥabbah* [friendship/loving] and I have yet to see anyone provide an essential definition. This is because such a definition is inconceivable; one can only speak of its effects and correlations. This incapacity is enhanced by the fact that God has attributed the attribute to Himself.[1]

Gnostics become very excited when they encounter terms referring to attributes which God has assigned to himself.[2] The reason for this excitement may be found in the prophetic tradi-

---

[1] M. Ibn ʿArabī, *al-Futūḥāt al-Makkīyah* (Meccan Openings), vol. 2 (Beirut: Dār Iḥyāʾ al-Turāth al-ʾArabī Publications, 1996), p. 320.

[2] The author takes this opportunity to thank F. Fotouhi-Ghazvini for her comments and thoughts.

tion: "Verily God has created man in His own Image."[3] When God is "friendly" or "loving," this implies that no one else can independently be a friend; nevertheless, wayfarers—who will be content with *second* best—endeavor to incorporate this attribute within themselves. They want to discover their true identity through the divine attributes. On the reality of "friendship," Ibn Fanārī writes that "it is a matter of conscience and that which has been said with respect to its definition is nothing but some corollary and conventional matters."[4] How can it be defined in its entire truth when God alone is the sole friend and lover of all? Only through communion will one be able to witness such a reality and thereafter "be" such a reality.

In addition to the literal definition of friendship which is self-evident, the ethicists have formulated a technical definition based on the Scriptures, which reads:

> The truth of friendship lies in a relationship of unity which unites the lover with the beloved; there is a pull on behalf of the beloved that attracts the lover to it. In proportion to the extent of this pull (toward the beloved), a degree of the existence of the lover becomes eliminated. Hence there is a direct relationship between the beloved's pull and the lover's annihilation (in the beloved). After this pull is established, the beloved takes away the personal attributes of the lover. Thereafter, the beloved steals away the lover's essence and grants an essence that deserves to be in unity with His attributes.[5]

Hence, friendship is a two-way process involving God's pull and man's effort to strive toward that divine attraction. The expression of true and real friendship is to be found solely in relation

---

[3] M. Kulaynī, *Uṣūl al-Kāfī* (Compendium of Shiʿa Traditions), 4th ed., vol. 1 (Qum: Qāʾim Āle, Muhammad Publications, 2008), p. 288.

[4] M. Ibn Fanārī, *Miṣbāḥ al-Uns* (Light of Acquaintance) (Tehran: Mawlā Publications, 1995), p. 245.

[5] R. M. Khomeini, *Miṣbāḥ al-Hidāyah wa Miftāḥ al-Kifāyah* (Lamp of Guidance and Key to Sufficiency) (Qum: Institute for the Compilation and Preservation of Imam Khomeini's Works), p. 406.

to God, and the locus for this friendship is the heart, i.e., the locus for the manifestation of God's attributes. Only on detaching from other than God will one be able to acquire such a love toward God, seeing Him in all actions, attributes, and things. Loving other than God is a Gnostic's definition of betrayal. The heart can also refer to the reality of *fiṭrah*—the inborn book of existence written within us all—that, on becoming activated on a par with the divine canon, leads to one's communion with the Lord. By properly filling one's innate nature, one is enhancing one's inner pull toward absolute perfection. The further one travels along this infinite route, the more divine love one possesses and manifests. The less or the more improperly one writes in one's book, the more pseudo-love one acquires toward other than God, thus distancing oneself more and more from the true source of all love. Differentiating between the domains of pure and impure love is the traveler's incentive, motivation, and intention.

Assuming one's ultimate aim in all things is to acquire affinity with God alone, one's friendship will be genuine—in relation to God, oneself, and others. However, if one's affinity is confined to God's manifestations *qua* manifestations, then the love that emanates from such a person does not lead to the building of relationships with either God, oneself, or others.

The Gnostics have provided protocols[6] for us to be able to differentiate between false and true love. With false, figurative love toward a thing or person, the cause of and incentive for one's growth and dynamism is tantamount to "being away" from the thing or person. Before attaining to the thing or person, one is constantly in motion and feels agitation. However, on acquiring the worldly and temporary thing or person, one gradually becomes more and more depressed, static, and motionless in relation to it. The road has come to a dead end. The exact opposite occurs on attaining unity with God, whose infinite and eternal manifestations lead one from moment to moment to states of

---

[6] ʿA. ʿAlamī, "Friendship and Love according to Imam Khomeini's Gnostic Trends," in *Collection of Works*, vol. 6 (Qum: Institute for the Compilation and Preservation of Imam Khomeini's Works, 2002): pp. 307–9.

"intoxication," "ecstasy," and "annihilation," always and forever longing for Him. Another parameter differentiating the two genres of love is that with the former, the main drive is toward one's ego, whereas with true love, the ego is eliminated.

In his ethical *magnum opus*, "Stations of the Wayfarers," Sheikh Abdullah Ansari (d. 481AH) has provided a protocol for those who are journeying toward God and have reached the station of "loving"—a protocol that has been elaborated on with commentary by ʿAbdul Razzāq Kāshānī (d. 736AH). In practical terms, on (a) donating one's self to the Beloved and (b) avoiding focus on the self (thus being attentive to the Beloved constantly), one will be attracted toward the Lord's everlasting grace and pull; it is only after accepting this grace, that one will qualify as a "friend" of God.[7] As is clear from the above prerequisites to friendship, one must start by eliminating the "I" and exiting the boundaries of one's ego. This truth has been alluded to esoterically in 4:100: "and whoever exits his home migrating towards God and His Messenger, and is then overtaken by death, his reward shall certainly fall on Allah." Exiting one's home refers to the exiting of one's ego, and being overtaken by death means total detachment from other than God.[8] At this stage, one cannot but choose God alone; this reality is depicted in the "Lovers' Supplication," where Imam Zayn al-ʿĀbidīn (fourth successor to the Holy Prophet) exclaims "Oh God! Is there anyone who will choose other than You after having tasted the sweetness of [Your] friendship."[9]

Kāshāni[10] then lays out his tripartite classification. At the first level, as a result of one's total focus on God in all matters, three signs arise. First, temptations and doubts begin to disappear.

---

[7] ʿA. Kāshānī, *Commentary to "Stations of the Wayfarers"* (Qum: Āyat Ishrāq Publications, 2008), pp. 217–18.

[8] R. M. Khomeini, *Ādābe Namāz* (Etiquettes of Prayer), 17th ed. (Qum:Institute for the Compilation and Preservation for Imam Khomeini's Works, 2010), pp.161–62.

[9] *Mafātīḥ al-Jinān* (A Collection of Prayers and Supplications), comp. A. Qummī (Qum: Nashtā Publications, 2010), p. 214.

[10] ʿA. Kāshānī, *Commentary to "Stations of the Wayfarers,"* p. 218–19.

From action to action, one dedicates one's action and oneself more and more to God. It is not about "me" anymore; it is all about God and manifesting God—a manifestation that lies deep down—the essence of one's identity.

Second, one acquires pleasure from executing commitments and working hard in God's name. The more one is in need of a given source of provision, the more love one expresses toward it. Imagine that the source is forever gracious and eternally compassionate. One's inner drive toward the most demanding of actions will be incessant.

Third, one experiences total relief and composure when burdens are heavy. However, it must be noted that true lovers—those whose only affinity is toward God—would never speak of any event or task as a "burden." What people ordinarily refer to as burdens are received by the lover with ecstasy, for the lover sees God in everything.

In relation to the mechanism of mastering the first level and manifesting such attributes, Kāshānī suggests three instructions.[11] First, studying, analyzing, and expressing constant gratitude for all the innumerable favors one has been blessed with by God. "He has showered upon you His blessings, the outer and the inner ones" (31:20). The more one thanks x, the more one recalls x; the more one recalls something, the more one acquires affinity toward it.

Then, one abides by the perfect exemplars. According to one's life, actions, speech, etc., this involves being on a par with the divine Prophets who are complete manifestations of God's attributes. As we read in 3:31, "Say [Oh Muhammad say to them]: If you want to love God, then follow me; God will then love you." This abiding may either be obligatory (i.e., where the Canon necessitates a particular action, e.g., the five daily prayers for Muslims, or the Sunday Mass for Catholics) or recommended.

Finally, one expresses utter neediness when executing the required rituals and protocols and never attributes good deeds

---

[11] Ibid.

to oneself. In short, one must see oneself as lowly, needy, and desperately dependent on God. As the Qur'an states in 35:15, "Oh Man! You are nothingness [moving] towards God and He is the all-sufficient and all-praiseworthy." In a sacred tradition, God has said, "Oh servant! Assign your sins under your feet [acknowledging hatred in relation to it] and assign your good deeds under your sins [expressing detachment from it even more; after all, attributing of virtue to oneself is more of a threat to the 'I' than being a sinner]." [12] In another sacred tradition, God has said, "Whoever I love, I shall kill [i.e., divine love destroys all traces of one's ego]; and whoever I kill, their blood money is upon me, and whoever's blood money is upon me, I am the blood money." [13]

There are three signs to look out for in the second and loftier level of friendship. [14] The first is choosing God over others in all affairs; filling one's heart with God's love leaves no room for other than God. 33:4 reads, "God has not put two hearts in anyone." Many however divert their love to other than Allah. With regard to these people, 2:165-166 reads, "Among the people are those who set up compeers besides Allah, loving them as if loving Allah—but the faithful have a more ardent love for Allah." In this equilibrium of love and friendship, the believer is one whose love for Allah at least predominates over one's love for other than Allah. In 9:24 the fate of choosing other than God over God is noted:

> Say, if your fathers and your sons, your brethren, your spouses and your kinsfolk, the possessions that you have acquired, the trade you fear may suffer, and the dwellings you are fond of, are dearer to you than Allah and His Apostle and to waging jihad in His way, then wait until Allah issues His verdict and Allah does not guide the transgressing lot.

[12] E. M. Larijani, *A Commentary on Ansārī's "Stations of the Wayfarers,"* 2nd ed. (Tehran: Sepehr Publications, 2012), p. 409.

[13] F. Kāshānī, *Qurrat al-ʾAyn*, p. 366.

[14] ʿA. Kāshānī, *Commentary to "Stations of the Wayfarers,"* p. 221.

On the same theme, Imam Ṣādiq has said, "Faith will not become complete and refined until one is more friendly toward God than one is to one's self, father, mother, offspring, family, capital and to all people."[15]

The second sign is verbally recalling God (through mantras etc.) as a result of the constant presence of the divine within you. As Imam Ali put it, "Whoever likes something, recalls it a lot."[16]

The third sign is wholeheartedly desiring to see one's beloved in all matters, i.e., observing God as the cause of all things. God is the quencher when you drink, the nourisher when you eat, the protector when you set your alarm, the provider when you visit the grocers, the healer when you are at the clinic, etc.

The route to acquiring these attributes entails the following mechanisms of action:[17]

First, deliberating carefully over God's attributes: a proper understanding of His attributes prevents one from acquiring spiritual illness. By way of example, fully becoming familiar with the fact that God is all-wise, omnipresent and all-forgiving leaves no room for jealousy, insolence, and grudges.

Then, deliberating over creation: creation by definition is the sign that reflects God. Preoccupying yourself in things that do not act as your route to God is tantamount to living a futile life. This truth is delicately phrased in 2:164:

> Indeed in the creation of the heavens and the earth, and the alternation of night and day, and the ships that sail at sea, which profit to men, and the water that God sends down from the sky—with which He revives the earth after its death, and scatters therein every kind of animal—and the changing of the winds, and the clouds disposed between the sky and the earth, are surely *signs* for a people who apply reason.

---

[15] M.B. Majlisī, *Biḥār al-Anwār* (Ocean of Lights), vol. 70 (Beirut: Dār Iḥyāʾ al-Turāth al-ʾArabī Publications, 1983), p. 25.

[16] *al-Mīzān al-Ḥikmah* (Compendium of Shiʿa Traditions) comp. M. Reyshahri, vol. 2 (Qum: Dār al-Ḥadīth Publications, 2004), p. 936.

[17] ʿA. Kāshānī, *Commentary to "Stations of the Wayfarers,"* pp. 221–22.

And finally, practicing asceticism by suppressing[18] or at least controlling one's nutritional and sexual appetites and also reducing one's socializing, talking on matters other than one's beloved, etc.

The third stage of friendship has three further signs.[19] First, one's intellect becomes latent. Here, as a result of becoming more and more God-like, incorporating the divine attributes leads to one's becoming enamored by God. Such a state of annihilation leaves no room for the intellect. A second sign is conveying and receiving matters in the shortest time and quickest manner. The third sign is acquiring unity with God's essence and not being held back even by the divine attributes. That is to say, one sees God in all things, rather than seeing things as a route and reflection of God. As we read in the Qur'an, "He is the first and the last, the outer and the inner" (57:3), and "He is with you wherever you are" (57:4).

Abraham and the Four Birds

In 2:260, the Qur'an tells the following story of Abraham and the four birds:

> And when Abraham said, "My Lord! Show me how You revive the dead," He said, "Do you not believe?" Abraham replied, "Yes indeed, but in order that my heart be at rest." He said, "Take four birds; then cut them into pieces and place a part of them on every mountain and then call upon them; they will come to you hastening."

Prophet Abraham was a complete manifestation of God's attributes. He has been assigned the title of God's friend (*khalīlullāh*) due to his mastering all the degrees of love and friendship.

---

[18] In 5:82, the Qur'an says, "and surely you will find the nearest of them in affection to the faithful to be those who say 'we are Christians'; that is because amongst them are men devoted to learning and who have renounced the world and because they are not arrogant."

[19] ʿA. Kāshānī, *Commentary to "Stations of the Wayfarers,"* p. 222.

Prophets are intermediaries between God and creation. They manifest divine attributes in addition to being human beings. As a result of acting as such a medium between God and creation, they take human queries to God and relate God's protocols to humanity. They are God's representatives on earth as well as the representatives of humankind in the divine realm.[20]

There are many interpretations—exoteric and esoteric—of this Qur'anic story. Stories in the Qur'an possess layers of esoteric meanings usually focusing on how to eliminate one's ego. These meanings should not, however, lead one to negate the exoteric angles portrayed in the verse. According to some traditions,[21] Abraham knew that whoever becomes adept at *khullat* (intense friendship) will be able to execute divine powers, even that of reviving the dead. Hence he asked to "see" *how* the dead are revived and was shown it. Although the common understanding among theologians and Gnostics is that the revival of the birds occurred in this physical realm of existence, some Gnostics put forth the idea that such an event was in fact an immaterial apparition.[22] This point however is beyond the scope of this article.

An important esoteric understanding taken from this story is that Abraham, as an intermediary between God and human beings, had come before God with the people's desire to know how one must live in order to acquire tranquility of the heart. On spiritually ascending, and thus transcending, different realms of existence, Abraham unveils divine immaterial data that are later converted into images of intuition (like the semi-immaterial images we experience in our dreams). These images of four birds—peacock, vulture, rooster, and crow—are God's

[20] F. Tabataba'ī, *A Word on Love: Ibn 'Arabī and Imam Khomeini's Perspectives* (Tehran: Imam Khomeini and Islamic Revolution Academy Publications, 2009), pp. 119–20.

[21] *Nūr al-Thaqalayn* (Tradition-based Exegesis of the Holy Qur'an) comp. 'A. Huwayzī, vol. 1 (Qum: Navīd Islam Publications, 2010), p. 596.

[22] 'A. Ardabīlī, *Taqrīrāt Falsafiye Imām Khumaynī* (Lecture Notes of Imam Khomeini's Philosophy Teachings) vol. 3 (Qum: Institute for the Compilation and Preservation of Imam Khomeini's Works, 2011), p. 591.

response to the human request given to their representative. Each of these birds possesses the attributes of a specific vice. The peacock is known for its love of itself, and thus for its arrogance. The vulture consumes dead flesh, which indicates its gross absorption in materialism. The rooster is sexually overactive, while the crow is gluttonous. The order to cut them into pieces may refer to the fact that humans must slaughter these vices within themselves before being able to acquire tranquility of heart, which is on par with the state of intense friendship with God.[23]

This idea of "friendship" plays an essential role for monks and mullahs who have chosen to follow such prophets by imitating their way of life. If one is to revive a static, dead people, one must be a true friend of God and acquire the tranquility of heart that makes it possible to communicate with, understand, and guide others. The Abrahamic model teaches us the necessary spiritual features one would need to attain in order to do this. Prophet Jesus—also regarded as the spirit of God—would exoterically revive the dead and also esoterically revive their hearts. This more important esoteric revival can be observed in Matthew 5:38-42[24] and Luke 6:27-31.[25] As with the teaching of Jesus, the Prophet Muhammad's protocol also is based on love. As he has said, according to one tradition, "My basis of action is love."[26] Love, in

---

[23] *Nūr al-Thaqalayn*, vol.1, p. 596.

[24] You have heard that it was said, "An eye for an eye and a tooth for a tooth." But I say to you, do not resist an evildoer. But if anyone strikes you on the right cheek, turn the other also; and if anyone wants to sue you and take your coat, give your cloak as well; and if anyone forces you to go one mile, go also the second mile. Give to everyone who begs from you, and do not refuse anyone who wants to borrow from you.

[25] But I say to you that listen, Love your enemies, do good to those who hate you, bless those who curse you, pray for those who abuse you. If anyone strikes you on the cheek, offer the other also; and from anyone who takes away your coat do not withhold even your shirt. Give to everyone who begs from you; and if anyone takes away your goods, do not ask for them again. Do to others as you would have them do to you.

[26] M. Nūrī, *Mustadrak al-Wasā ʾil* (Compendium of Shiᶜa Traditions), vol.11 (Qum:Āl-ul Bayt Publications, 1986), p. 173.

its varying degrees of manifestation, is always the first course of action, enabling people to accept the divine message in their hearts. The divine message must come from a pure heart that manifests divine attributes such as love, compassion, mercy, etc.

The ultimate principle of "being *God's* friend before befriending other than God" is universal in all monotheistic religions. There are many sacred traditions in which the Holy Prophet narrates conversations between God and different messengers. These traditions illustrate the positive consequences that emanate from those who have acquired true friendship with God. Two of these traditions have to do with conversations with Prophets Moses and David:

> Oh Moses! One who claims to love me but sleeps at night without recalling me, is in fact lying. Is it not the case that that lovers desire solitude with their beloved? Oh Moses, I am aware of the states of my friends; when the night time embraces them, I shall make them see from their hearts and let them see my punishment. They shall see Me and speak to me! Oh Moses! Be humble at heart towards Me and bodily subservient. Cry during the darkness of the night and call upon Me for you will perceive Me as close to you and as answering your call."[27]

> Oh David! . . . be humble and subservient towards your people; concerning those who will God [desiring to get close to Him], do not be difficult with them. If My lovers only knew the high status those who desire to get close to Me have before Me, they [God's friends/lovers] would have assigned themselves as the earth upon which those people tread."[28]

[27] M.T. Miṣbāḥ, "Significance of Friendship," *Marifat Journal* 21, no. 5 (2012): p. 7

[28] Ibid., p. 6.

Ora et Labora

Muhammad Legenhausen

Dialogue requires common language, and so we use English as the contemporary "language of conferences." To enrich our dialogue, however, we need to enrich our linguistic abilities. We need to learn one another's languages, or at least a few expressions. So, I would like to offer a few words of Latin, Arabic, and Persian.

The monastic life, especially in the Benedictine tradition, is often described by the phrase, *ora et labora* (pray and work). Here *ora* has the same root as the English words *orate* (L. *orāt-*, ppl. stem of *ōrāre* to speak, plead, pray, and oral, from L. *ōs, ōr-* mouth). The English word *labor* comes by way of French from the Latin root *labōrem*: labor, toil, distress, trouble. The verbal form gives us *labora*. So, the monastic life is one of speaking and suffering, saying prayers and working, and, I would propose, evangelizing and toiling. (I will come back to this.)

The phase *ora et labora* does not occur in the sixth century *Rule of Saint Benedict*.[1] It has been traced to the late medieval period.[2]

---

[1] For a translation of the *Rule* in English as well as links to other translations and a wealth of other information, see "The Rule of St. Benedict Arranged by Chapter Titles," accessed August 16, 2013, http://www.osb.org/rb/text/index.html.

[2] See "Mönchtum im Abendland: Bete und Arbeite," accessed August 16, 2013, http://universal_lexikon.deacademic.com/274417/M%C3%B6nchtum_im_Abendland%3A_Bete_und_arbeite.

Benedictines have explained that if we analyze the life prescribed by Saint Benedict's *Rule,* there are three daily activities prescribed for the monasteries: prayer, work, and reading (*lectio*). Accordingly, a more appropriate motto would be *ora et labora et lege,*[3] where *lege* means *read.* Some Benedictines have also expressed dissatisfaction with the emphasis on work when understood too narrowly; one should not give the impression that the monastery is a labor camp![4] While we should recognize, therefore, the reasons some Benedictines may have reservations about the phrase, it may nevertheless serve some purposes of Benedictine/Shi'a dialogue.[5] If understood broadly, the call to prayer and work may be seen as one in which study and reading combine elements of both as a realization of the interweaving of faith and good works. As a Benedictine sister puts it, "Saint Benedict describes a fairly seamless garment of faith and works for us to weave and wear."[6]

In Islam there is also an emphasis on a life in which faith and good works are interwoven.[7] Consider Sura 103 of the Qur'an:

---

[3] This motto is used to head the Austrian Benedictine website "Ora et Labora et Lege: Bete und Arbeite und Lese," accessed August 13, 2013, http://www.stiftmelk.at/pfarren/oraetlabora.html; for reflections on the importance of reading in the *Rule,* see P. Amadeus Hörschläger, "Morgengedanken aus der Regel des hl. Benedikt,"accessed August 16, 2013, www.eduhi.at/dl/EB-07-Amadeus-Morgengedanken.doc; *also see Casey Bailey, "Lectio Divina," accessed August 16, 2013,* http://trappistabbey.org/?page_id=600; See Terrence Kardong, "Work is Prayer: Not!", accessed August 16, 2013, http://www.osb.org/gen/topics/work/kard1.html.

[4] See Linda Kulzer, "Monastic Life as the Community's Primary Work," accessed August 16, 2013, http://www.osb.org/gen/topics/work/kulzer.html.

[5] I am grateful to William Skudlarek for bringing to my attention some of the issues that have been raised about the phrase "ora et labora."

[6] Virginia Jung. "Reflections on Isaiah 50:5-9a; Psalms 116:1-2, 3-4, 5-6, 8-9; James 2:14-18; Mark 8:27-35," accessed August 13, 2013, http://www.osbchicago.org/Sept16_2012SunReflJung.htm.

[7] For some reflections on common attitudes among Benedictines and Anabaptists on the issue of faith and good works, see Eoin de Bhaldraithe,

In the Name of Allah, the Compassionate the Merciful

By the age

Surely man is lost

Except those who believe and work righteousness and enjoin the Truth and enjoin patience.[8]

This sura is linguistically exquisite; its beauty is hidden by the translation. First, consider ʿasr: it is the age, the time, but also the afternoon, or the decline of the day: the time that fades away and passes. God does a lot of swearing in the Qurʾan—not by using foul language, but by appealing to human beings through signs and symbols conveyed in beautiful words, such as: "By the break of day" (89:1), "By the sky" (85:1), "By the moon" (74:32), "By the pen" (68:1), "By the fig and the olive" (95:1), among others. In this sura, God swears by the age, that is, by the declining time, that human beings are lost, or, more literally, in a loss, khusr. The sense of the Arabic is not of having lost one's way (although this is not to be denied), but of having suffered an irretrievable loss in one's commerce. It is said that if the cloth merchant suffers a loss in trade, at least his cloth remains to be sold the next day. If the ice seller is unable to sell his merchandise in time, however, he suffers an irretrievable loss. So, there is a sense of decline in both the concepts of *time* or *the age* and *loss*. Surely, human beings come out as losers, and irretrievably so, except for those who believe, those who have faith, imān, and those who do or work good deeds. To do or work is ʿamila, meaning *he worked, wrought, labored, served, did service, did, acted, performed*, and, according to Lane's lexicon, it is often used for actions that are done with some difficulty, or with intention. It

---

"Michael Sattler, Benedictine and Anabaptist," *Downside Review*, 105 (1987): 111–31. It is to be noted that there has been considerable prayer and work between Shiʿa and Mennonites and Benedictines and Mennonites. Perhaps the common attitude toward faith and good works may be seen as an element that facilitates the ensuing friendships.

[8] Translation by the author.

seems to provide a good translation for the Latin *labora*. The labor that is commended in the Qurʾan to avoid loss when coupled with faith is *ṣāliḥāt*, usually translated as *good deeds*; but it is to be noted that *peace*, in the sense of a *peace treaty*, is also translated into Arabic with the same root: *ṣulḥ*. Faith and good works are finally coupled with the promotion of the Truth, *Ḥaqq*, which is what is right as well as true (*Ḥaqq* is also one of the Names of Allah), and patience, *ṣabr*. The constancy of the right, the true, and patience is thus contrasted with the declining nature of time and loss.

Although we worship the same God, and although our religious lives share many common elements and aims, Christians and Muslims have often seen one another as enemies. Unfortunately, many Christians and Muslims continue to see one another as enemies today. As we Shiʿa Muslims and Benedictine Catholic Christians come together in friendship and dialogue, we may set our hopes with another Benedictine motto: *pax* (peace).[9] Like many other concepts in both Christianity and Islam, *Pax* is one that can be found in the pagan culture, for when Augustus founded the Roman Empire in 27 BCE, he was said to have established the *Pax Romana* or *Pax Augusta*. He established *Pax* as a Roman goddess, the daughter of Jupiter and Iustitia. Christianity rejected the pagan gods and goddesses and called Christ the *Princeps Pacis*, after the Hebrew, *sar shalom*, of Isaiah 9:6.

The ideal of peace is also one that characterizes Islam. Our greeting, "*salām ʿalaykum*," is a prayer for peace, and the heavenly reward is characterized as the abode of peace, *dār al-salām*:

> That is the straight path of *your* Lord. We have already elaborated the signs for a people who take admonition. For them shall be the abode of peace [*dār al-salām*] near their Lord, and

---

[9] Both *"Ora et Labora"* and *"Pax"* are presented as mottoes by the Missionary Sisters of St. Benedict (Illinois, USA), accessed August 13, 2013, http://missionarysisosb.org/oraetlabora/.

He will be their guardian because of what they used to do.
(6:126-127)[10]

In what follows, I invite reflection on the connection between these two Benedictine mottos: *Ora et labora* and *Pax*, how these ideas figure in Islamic thought, and how they may help to further our work of dialogue.

Evangelization

The term *evangelist* comes from *evangelium*, which is the Latin for the Greek, *euanggelon* bringing good news, from *eu* well + *anggelein* to announce. The "good news" that is brought is the news of the Kingdom of God. I would suggest that the Kingdom of God preached by Christ is the *dar al-salam* mentioned in the *ayah* of the Qurʾan above. The first four books of the New Testament are called the gospels because they convey the teaching of Christ, the teaching of the kingdom of God. It is that same teaching which, according to Muslims, was revealed to Christ by divine revelation. It is called the *Injīl* in the Glorious Qurʾan.[11]

> He forgives whomever He wishes, and punishes whomever He wishes, and to Allah belongs the kingdom of the heavens and the earth, and whatever is between them, and toward Him is the return. O People of the Book! Certainly Our Apostle has come to you, clarifying for you after a gap in the apostles, lest you should say, "There did not come to us any bearer of good

[10] For further discussion on peace in the Qurʾan, see the article by my colleagues Mohammad Ali Shomali and Mahmud Mohammadi Araghi, "Peace: A Qurʾanic Perspective," in *Peace and Justice: Essays from the Fourth Shiʿi Muslim Mennonite Christian Dialogue*, eds. Harry J. Huebner and Muhammad Legenhausen (Winnipeg: CMU Press, 2011), pp. 144–50.

[11] For a more detailed exploration of this theme, see Muhammad Legenhausen, "Jesus as *Kalimat Allah*, the Word of God," in *Word of God*, ed. Mohammad Ali Shomali (London: Institute of Islamic Studies, Islamic Centre of England, 2009), pp. 129–56.

news nor any warner." Certainly there has come to you a bearer
of good news and a warner. And Allah has power over all
things. (5:18-19)

Muslims and Christians are both called upon to preach the
good news of the kingdom of God. There is much in common
between Christian and Islamic teachings about the divine kingdom, including the fact that in both traditions, there is considerable ambiguity on what the kingdom is. Believers, whether
Christian or Muslim, are asked to repent of their sins, to follow
divine instruction, and live virtuously. They are promised that
if they do so, they will be rewarded, and that they ignore the
divine message at their own peril. That is the warning.

Christian evangelization has become an area of contention
between Christians and Muslims. Christians are generally not
free to seek converts in Muslim countries, and evangelization is
commonly misunderstood to mean seeking converts. Christian
evangelization is in fact seen by many Christians as well as Muslims as being the attempt to win Muslims away from their religion and sign them up as members of the church. So, instead of
seeking to help people to find the way to the Kingdom of God,
helping them to live virtuous lives in accordance with divine
teachings, we find religious people fighting among themselves
about the best way to bring about the peace that religion
promises.

According to the teachings of the Catholic Church, however,
there is a much clearer and truer understanding of evangelism.
It goes back to its original meaning of bringing the "good news"
taught by Christ, and includes dialogue as a way of carrying out
this divine obligation. In this, we, as Muslims and Christians,
are able to participate in evangelization together. This is not to
neglect the fact that we still have differences. Muslims and Christians differ about the implications of the good news, about what
Christ taught, who he was, and what one must do to follow his
way. Needless to say, Christians differ among themselves about
these questions, as well. But a conception of evangelization that
places dialogue and cooperation at the forefront deserves more

attention by Christians and Muslims alike, and may assist in overcoming some of the tensions in our wider communities.

The following words are from a published talk by Archbishop Michael L. Fitzgerald at a workshop for American Benedictine Abbots held at the Prince of Peace Benedictine Monastery in Oceanside, California, from January 29 to 31, 2005. They provide an entryway into the church's understanding of the relationship between evangelization and interreligious dialogue.

> "Interreligious dialogue is a part of the Church's evangelizing mission" (RM 55). This clear statement, found in John Paul II's missionary encyclical *Redemptor Hominis* (1990), recognizes the important role of interreligious dialogue in the Church's life. This was not a new idea, since it already appears in the documents of the Second Vatican Council. Recent Popes have developed the bare outlines of these documents, and Paul VI's journeys and John Paul II's visits, talks, and teachings have emphasized the importance of relations with people from other religious traditions.[12]

In the talk, Archbishop Fitzgerald continues by drawing on church documents to outline some varieties of interreligious dialogue: The *dialogue of life*, where people strive to live in an open and neighborly spirit, sharing their joys and sorrows, their human problems and preoccupations; the *dialogue of action*, in which Christians and others collaborate for the integral development and liberation of people; the *dialogue of theological exchange*, where specialists seek to deepen their understanding of their respective religious heritage, and to appreciate each other's spiritual values; the *dialogue of religious experience*, where persons rooted in their own religious traditions share their spiritual riches, for instance with regard to prayer and contemplation, faith and ways of searching for God or the Absolute.

---

[12] Archbishop Michael L. Fitzgerald, MA, "The Catholic Church and Interreligious Dialogue" *Bulletin of Monastic Interreligious Dialogue*, 75 (October 2005), http://monasticdialog.com/a.php?id=723.

Pax

Archbishop Fitzgerald quotes from *Dialogue and Proclamation* to demonstrate the link between dialogue and peace: "There is need also to join together in trying to solve the great problems facing society and the world, as well as in education for justice and peace."[13] He finishes his talk with another quote from *Dialogue and Proclamation*:

> It must be remembered that the Church's commitment to dialogue is not dependent on success in achieving mutual understanding and enrichment; rather it flows from God's initiative in entering into dialogue with humankind and from the example of Jesus Christ whose life, death and resurrection gave to that dialogue its ultimate expression.[14]

Despite, our theological differences, there is a good foundation on which to build that has been set by the writers of *Dialogue and Proclamation* and Archbishop Fitzgerald. The full title of the document from which Archbishop Fitzgerald drew parts of his talk is *Dialogue and Proclamation: Reflection and Orientations on Interreligious Dialogue and the Proclamation of the Gospel of Jesus Christ*. It was jointly issued in May, 1991, by the Pontifical Council for Inter-Religious Dialogue and the Congregation for the Evangelization of Peoples. Its stated goal was the further consideration of dialogue and proclamation in the evangelizing mission of the church.

Some observers consider this document to be a high point in the advance toward dialogue on the part of the church, and that, in the ten years following, the tone has somewhat soured.[15] From our own very limited perspective, such a judgment would be premature. The flourishing of dialogue cannot be judged by a survey of the "tone" of various documents issued by diverse

[13] Ibid.

[14] Ibid.

[15] See Mark Plaiss, "'Dialogue and Proclamation' a Decade Later: A Retreat?" *Journal of Ecumenical Studies*, vol. 38, nos. 2–3 (Summer–Fall 2001).

ecclesiastical bodies. Many of our Muslim colleagues also express suspicions about dialogue and are unwilling to give serious consideration to interreligious cooperation. The biggest obstacles to increased amity do not come from our dialogue partners, but from the dialogue skeptics in our own communities. So, if we are to move in the direction of peace and amity beyond our own group, we have much work to do.

Labora

The work of dialogue with one another may turn out to be easier than the work of reassuring dialogue skeptics in our own communities. I invite reflection on "Towards Reforming the International Financial and Monetary Systems in the Context of Global Public Authority," by the Pontifical Council for Justice and Peace, which was issued in October 2011. I believe that the proposals made in this document are entirely in keeping (or very nearly so) with Islamic views on the subject. I read a summary of the document in Persian for Ayatullah Mesbah Yazdi, who immediately suggested that the document be translated into Persian. He expressed hopes that it would receive attention among our scholars and perhaps stimulate comparable work on our part. I am happy to be able to report that the work has been translated and published (in a journal edited by Dr. Shomali, *Maᵓrifat Adiyan*) with an introduction by a former student, Morteza Saneᵓi.[16] The reaction to this publication has not led to a wave of interest from the seminaries of Qum in cooperation with the church on this issue. Maybe it is too early for that. In any case, this is just an example of the sort of work that I think Catholics and Shiᶜa can engage in as a part of the dialogue of action, although the work of overcoming suspicions and reticence

---

[16] Morteza Saneᵓi., "An Introduction to the Statement Issued by the Pontifical Council for Justice and Peace on the Current Global Economic and Financial Crisis," trans. Sayyid Rahim Rastitabar, *Maᵓrifat Adiyan*, no. 6, 1390/2012.

may be no less daunting than the work of reforming the world financial system!

The following suggestions come to mind: a wider diversity of our colleagues should become involved in dialogue; proceedings and reports of interreligious efforts should be more widely publicized within our communities through newsletters and websites, as well as journals; practical forms of cooperation, or *dialogue of action*, should be given greater attention; perhaps we could pair communities of specific monasteries with institutions in Qum, in the style of sister cities; we should offer one another resources—at the very least the ability to have questions answered about our respective institutions, beliefs, etc., through e-mail, visits, short courses, learning tours, etc.; and finally, we should pray for divine aid in our attempts to do His will through dialogue.

Ora

We are members of prayerful communities, but our worship takes very different forms. While much worship is only possible within one's own religious community, there are forms of prayer that can be conducted in concert with those with whom we have theological, political, and other types of differences.

Saint Teresa Benedicta of the Cross, or Edith Stein, made a very important point in her early writings on empathy. One can feel with another person, empathize with that person, without having his or her feeling as one's own. So, to use her example, when I see the happiness of my little brother at seeing our mother after an absence, I feel that happiness of his with him. At the same time, I need not be particularly happy about seeing our mother, or even about him seeing our mother. I think there is an important point here for our fellowship. We do not have to accept the beliefs and rules of one another to be able to empathize with the beliefs and obedience of our colleagues of other faiths. The human heart has a capacity for empathy that is not dependent on sameness or agreement. We can appreciate the worth of an act done or doctrine held by our brothers and sisters of other faiths without taking doctrines over as our own, without saying, "Oh, this is just like something else that we have," or, "This can be interpreted in a manner that is acceptable to us, too." We can recognize some truths as foreign truths, even without any hope or attempt to domesticate them.

So, we can pray together, in the sense of supplicating God and reading or listening to one another's Scriptures, without any consideration of what agrees with and what does not agree with our own ways, because we can empathize with one another's prayers. This does have limits, however. As Muslims, we cannot become communicants, after all! And Christians are not permitted to perform the Hajj. We are different communities, with different ways and beliefs. There are fascinating similarities and insuperable differences, which are both perfectly compatible with our ability to find ourselves as individuals and as communities coming to love one another in many of the varied senses of friendship that have been explicated and explored by our colleagues during the two days of this symposium.

Hafez

The following *ghazal* of Hafez speaks to our issues, often in ways that may seem to rub against the grain of what I have been trying to say.

> *The produce of the workshop of the cosmos—it's not everything!*
> *Bring the wine! For the furnishings of the world—it's not everything!*
>
> *From heart and soul to have the honor of conversation with souls—*
>   *that's the point;*
> *that is everything; and, if not, heart and soul—it's not everything!*
>
> *For the sake of shade, do not oblige yourself to the Sidra and the Tuba*
>   *trees*[17]
> *For, O moving cypress, when you look well—it's not everything!*

[17] Trees of heaven.

Felicity is that which comes to one's side without heart's blood;
And, if not, (what is gained through) effort and toil of the garden of
the Beloved—it's not everything!

The five day reprieve that you have at this stage
Enjoy it well for a time, for time—it's not everything!

We are waiting at the lip of the ocean of annihilation, O Saki!
Know the opportunity, for from lip to mouth—it's not everything!

My suffering, the burning of weeping and wailing,
Apparently, the need for narrating and explaining—it's not
*   everything!*

Ascetic! beware; be not secure in the play of the cincture,
For the way from the cloister to the temple of the Magians—it's not
*   everything!*

The name of Hafez accepted the mark of excellence, however,
For the rascals, the mark of profit or loss—it's not everything![18]

I've been arguing that if we want to achieve peace and deepen our friendships, we should follow the Benedictine motto of prayer and work, *ora et labora*. Hafez says that whatever you can achieve by hard work and piety is nothing. He seems to think that the real success is that which just falls in our laps out of the blue; and that therefore we need not get too excited about what harvest we may reap through our labors. He also says that there is not so much distance between the monastery of the ascetic and the Zoroastrian temple. Hafez never misses a chance to take a swipe at false piety. The monastery and asceticism are always symbols of *false* piety for Hafez, while the Zoroastrian temple is the tavern where the wine of divine love is poured outside the confines of religious legitimacy. That divine love should be symbolized with wine should not be very foreign to our Christian

---

[18] Author's translation. Another translation was made by the well-known American poets Robert Bly and Leonard Lewisohn: *The Angels Knocking on the Tavern Door: Thirty Poems by Hafez* (New York: HarperCollins, 2008), 9–10.

friends—but here the idea of the wine of divine love is not the blood of Christ, but the wine that makes one drunk to the point of forgetting the self as one attends to the Beloved.

I think we can all go along with Hafez in saying that it is not our work and prayers alone through which anything is achieved, and his claim that what is important is what you don't work for can be revised as a reminder that all success depends on the grace (*lutf*) of God. But that does not mean, as Hafez seems to suggest, that we should just sit back and enjoy life while we trust in fate. We should pray and work, even as we realize that what is achieved is by His will and not brought about by our prayers and labors. Despite my disagreement with Hafez (which might well be caused by my own misunderstanding of him), I can appreciate his point, and see it as a pearl in the necklace of his poem.

As for false piety, pride is a particular danger for all who would lead a religious life. Philosophers are also especially susceptible to the sin of pride, as can be easily observed by attending any major philosophical conference. So, for those of us who attempt to travel the way of philosophy as a kind of religious life, the dangers are doubled, and the jibes of Hafez should not go unheeded.

Regarding the monastery and the cloister, however, I would like to suggest that we reflect on the line that says that they are not so far apart by considering how each of our cloisters, the Benedictine monastery and the *hawzah* of Qum, are not so far apart, even though it is common for many of those at home in either to view the other as outside the bounds of religious legitimacy.

What is truly important, Hafez says, is to be in the company of the souls, to have conversation, dialogue, from which I would conclude that what is important is that we are able to share in the company of one another as we pray and work for peace.

Postscript

In the Name of God, the All-Merciful, the Most Merciful

From the cold (-17 degrees Celsius) but at the same time shining surroundings of Montreal, I am very pleased to be able to share with our dear readers some of the experiences that my Christian and Muslim friends and I had while participating in the fifth round of Catholic-Shi'a dialogue which took place from September 28 to October 3, 2012. Of course, it is not possible to expect words to fully convey those beautiful memories that have been glowing in our hearts and minds since then, especially if someone like me is to select those words.

The theme of the dialogue was "friendship." In the past, we had discussed different themes such as exploring our theological and spiritual traditions and sharing our resources in order to face the challenges of living a life of faith in the contemporary world during which we focused on family and education, reason and faith in theory and practice, ethics in today's society with particular reference to bioethics, business ethics, and environmental ethics and prayer. This time we decided to discuss friendship. The suggestion had come from Father William Skudlarek and later on in Qum he told us that the reason he had proposed this topic was a question I had asked a year previously when we visited the Pontifical Institute for Arabic and Islamic Studies (PISAI) in Rome. I had visited PISAI several times before, but at that time my question for our hosts was whether their graduates become friends of Islam.

I think the theme of friendship was very relevant and some-how more personal than our previous ones, but perhaps we needed all those past discussions to reach this point. I also think that God helped us not only to discuss the subject in an open, sincere, and honest way but also to experience it among our-selves in a very strong way. Everything that I have heard since then from the participants confirmed that they all felt and ex-perienced a genuine and powerful sense of friendship, some-thing which was far from being merely formal or superficial, something that you may not even experience with some of your own relatives or fellow Muslims or Christians.

Here I would like to refer to some of the participants' reflec-tions in order to help those who did not attend the dialogue to at least experience it a little in some way.

> The generous hospitality of our partners opened the doors of our mind and heart. This helped to foster and enhance our "inter-religious friendship" as we had decided to call our rela-tionship instead of "inter-religious dialogue," which sounds too intellectual. I was impressed by the serious religiosity of the people and the deep spirituality of our partners, furthermore by the many students living in Qum and the high quality of their studies. Qum is a kind of theological and spiritual power station. I was also surprised to see the Armenian Church in Esfahan, which is not only beautifully painted but also a sign of local tolerance. (Abbot Primate Notker)

> There was no doubt that this was one of the most exciting dia-logues that have taken place. First, because of its location. We were in Iran, Qum, working in the International Institute for Islamic Studies, for the first time. Second, because the topic, "friendship," had the effect of strengthening the friendship made the previous year in Rome, and third, because of the remarkable hospitality offered by our Shiʿa hosts for us over the days we were with them. From the Benedictine side there is a great sense of gratitude for what was provided. (Abbot Timothy Wright)

> In addition to sensing how much deeper the friendship became among all of us who participated in the conference, I also re-member the friendliness of people we would simply meet on

the street or at places we went to visit. We were obviously foreigners, and I think most people recognized that we were
Catholic monks and nuns. Almost always we would be asked
where we were from, and I expected that when I said I was from
the United States, I would sense a certain reserve. But never
once did that happen.

One of the most memorable experiences was when we went
to the Holy Shrine of Fatemeh Masoumeh. When we got there,
some of us walked into the large courtyard and then were called
back. I immediately thought that we had entered a space where
we weren't allowed. But, in fact, we were simply being asked
to wait for the imam who was head of the shrine to come from
his home to receive us. After a most gracious reception in the
parlor, we were taken to visit the tomb—we downstairs, the
women upstairs. When they rejoined us, Sisters Julian and Lucy
were almost in tears because they had been welcomed with
such affection.

In short, it would be hard for me to imagine a better place for
a Christian/Muslim dialogue on friendship than Iran! (Fr William
Skudlarek)

I think a great deal of friendship and informal dialogue was
fostered practically in the out-of-lecture times, our local sight-
seeing, our meals and travel together—including the long journey to Esfahan and back—our picnic at the Mountain of Elijah,
our times of prayer, all the educational and other visits. Some
of this was a "silent" dialogue and communication (as in our
prayer times together in IIS) united with each other in God, but
certainly for me it ALL deepened the sense of friendship and
community which began in the other conferences. (Sister Lucy
Brydon)

Travelling to Qum meant for me "meeting friends" (no difference if female or male). And the ground this friendship was
based on is God—our common confidence in God, His love and
His mercy. It was His spirit who worked among us. As we read
in the Bible: "if two or three meet in My name, I'll be among
them." And that is the deepest point, where people can meet in
friendship and in "dialogue." The rest means to listen, to experience, to understand, to explain, and so on. But the starting

point and the goal of the dialog is to meet in the face of God—
and this is the greatest present we got and we shared in Qom.
(Corinna Muehlsted)

When you can joyfully sit and eat together, meaningfully pray
together, and feel at home and close to God in one another's
holy sites, then surely you have really become intimate friends:

> What happened in both meetings in Rome and Qum and
> touched me more than just the content of the several papers we
> gave to one another is the hospitality in prayer and table. We
> were allowed to visit your shrines, to be witness of your prayer,
> even late at night inside the heart of the shrine, and at midday
> we were present to one another's moment of prayer, in silence
> or prayer of the heart, on depths that no one can measure except
> the One alone. Also the table community was impressive for
> me, even once inside the shrine again, but also once in family
> as it were on the hill, at late evening. These are gestures of
> profound esteem and true friendship, going further than articles
> and publications. And even when we were sharing papers, the
> quality of being interested to what the other from inside his or
> her tradition is exposing, brings hearts and minds closer to one
> another. Afterward we do speak about the other in a completely
> new way; one somehow has lived those moments of sharing on
> the three levels: study, prayer, and hospitality of the table.
> (Fr. Benoit Standaert)

It is, then, quite natural to think of sharing the Common Word
that you have been given by God with others, to think of the
ways in which you can work together to make the world a better
place for reflecting the light, beauty, and mercy of God:

> A word listened and prayed: the times of successive Muslim and
> Christian prayers were precious, and the silent participation we
> experienced opened to the Spring of all words. Even with little
> access to Arabic, words as "simple" as "Allahu Akbar"—espe-
> cially as they "took flesh" in your Muslim prayers—could open
> in my soul a path both known and unexpected. I felt clearly we
> could hear there a con-vocation (the fact of being called together)
> by the Unique God Who speaks to men, to each of us.

> A word to be shared: I remember as probably the greatest moments the visits of your spiritual shrines, especially the one of Hazrat Maʾsoumeh. The presence of our group in the middle of the crowd of pilgrims of all conditions reminded me, I guess, the horizon requested by the word we searched together, which is the whole humanity, all men and women, children and elderlies, people of all colours, whom the Creator of all calls to communion and harmony. (Br. Godefroy)

Perhaps we normally tend to think that friendship is at a level below family relationships; your friend can never be like your cousin, brother, sister, spouse, child, or parent. I think this might often be the case, but at the same time I think that friendship is such an intimate relationship that it can even be extended to include family members. Isn't it true that when we want to describe a very intimate relationship with, say, our parents, we say, "My mother or father is my best friend"? Among all people, your mother or father can be your best friend. We might even go beyond the human level and say, "God is my best friend," just as God also adopts some people as His friends. Thus the Qurʾan says, "God took Abraham for a friend" (4:125).

Now with great hope and high aspirations we look forward to our next dialogue, which will deal with the topic of community. I pray that in the same way God helped us to experience a deep sense of friendship, He would also help us to lay foundations for a community of the faithful. Or as Sister Julian wrote to me a few days ago:

> For the meeting in Assisi I hope we find a way of being a "community," even for only a few days. I believe it works wonders for a long time afterward. I also believe that it is this intensity of sharing that every participant takes home with him/her and radiates in his/her own community and surroundings; spoken and unspoken but always with this longing for a better, a shared world in honour of God The Almighty, in our souls.

I take this opportunity to thank God the Almighty once again for all His bounties and favours upon us, especially the gift of love and friendship, and beg Him not to leave us alone in our endeavours even for a single moment. As Imam Husayn, the martyred grandson of Prophet Muhammad, said:

> *O God, the one who does not have You what does he have?*
> *And the one who has You what does he lack?*

Mohammad Ali Shomali
17 December 2013

Selected Bibliographies

Chapter 2:
The Qur'an's Multifaceted Picture
of Muslim/Christian Relations

Armstrong, Karen. *Islam: A Short History*. London: Phoenix Press, 2004.

Ayoub, Mahmoud. *The Crisis of Muslim History: Religion and Politics of Early Islam*. Oxford: Oneworld, 2003.

Bell, Richard. *The Origin of Islam in its Christian Environment*. London: Frank Cass & Co. Ltd., 1968.

Burke, Jason. *Al-Qaeda: The True Story of Radical Islam*. Harlow, UK: Penguin Books, 2004

Pontifical Council for Interreligious Dialogue. *Interreligious Documents I: Guidelines for Dialogue between Christians and Muslims*. Prepared by Maurice Borrmans, translated by Marston R. Speight. New York: Paulist Press, 1990.

Casper, Robert. *A Historical Introduction to Islamic Theology: Muhammad and the Classical Period*. Rome: PISAI, 1998.

———. *Islamic Theology: Doctrines*. Rome: PISAI, 2007.

Ghrab, Saad. "Islam and Christianity: From Opposition to Dialogue." In Islamo-Christiana 13, 1985.

Ibn Hisham. *al-sira al-nabawiyya*, edited by Mustafa al-Saqqa et al. Cairo: sharika maktaba wa matba'a Mustafa al-babi al-halabi wa-'awladah bi-misr, 1955.

O'Mahony, Anthony, Wulstan Peterburs and Muhammad Ali Shomali, eds., *Catholic and Shi'a Dialogue: Studies in Theology and Spirituality.* London: Melisende, 2011.

Watt, Montgomery. *Muhammad's Mecca.* Edinburgh: Edinburgh University Press, 1988.

———. *Muhammad at Mecca.* Oxford, UK: Oxford University Press, 1953.

———. *Muhammad at Medina.* Oxford, UK: Oxford University Press, 1956.

Waquid (al-). *Kitab al-Maghazi.* Edited by Marsden J.B. Jones. 3 vols. Oxford, UK: Oxford University Press, 1966.

Chapter 6: A Monastic Approach to Friendship between Religions

Follon, Jacques, and James McEvoy, eds. *Sagesses de l'amitié I: Anthologie de textes philosophiques anciens* (Vestigia, no. 24) Fribourg/Paris: Cerf, 1997.

———. *Sagesses de l'amitié II. Anthologie de textes philosophiques patristiques, médiévaux et renaissants* (Vestigia, no. 29), Fribourg/Paris: Cerf, 2003.

Frère John de Taizé. *Une multitude d'amis. Réimaginer l'Église chrétienne à l'heure de la mondialisation.* Presses de Taizé, 2011.

Hyatte, Reginald. *The Arts of Friendship. The Idealization of Friendship in Medieval and Early Renaissance Literature.* New York: Brill Academic, 1997.

McGuire, Brian Patrick. *Friendship and Community: The Monastic Experience 350–1250* (Cistercian Studies no. 95). Kalamazoo, MI: Cistercian Publications, 1988.

List of Contributors

Godefroy Raguenet de Saint-Albin has been a Cistercian monk since 2001. He entered the Abbey of Notre-Dame d'Aiguebelle, the motherhouse of Tibhirine, as it was supporting an attempt (since interrupted) to re-found a community in Algeria. He has also lived with the Cistercian community of Atlas in Morocco on several occasions over the past four years.

Maximilian (Fredrick) Musindai is a monk of Prince of Peace-Tigoni, a Benedictine monastery in Kenya. He obtained a BA in sacred theology at the Pontifical Athenaeum S. Anselmo in Rome in 2009, and a licentiate in Arabic and Islamic Studies at the Pontifical Institute for Arabic and Islamic Studies (PISAI), also in Rome, in 2012. He is currently in Egypt preparing for the PhD program in Arabic and Islamic Studies at PISAI. His area of research is Relations between Christians and Muslims in history, at present, and in the future.

Timothy Wright, abbot emeritus of Ampleforth Abbey, UK, is currently the Abbot Primate's Delegate for Benedictine–Muslim Dialogue. While abbot, he, with Mohammad Ali Shomali, initi-ated the Benedictine-Shiʿa dialogue, which had three meetings in the UK. After a short period it was revived in Rome. While acting as a spiritual director at the Pontifical Beda College in Rome, he was able to undertake research on the relationship between the spirituality of the Rule of Benedict and the Qurʾan, eventually earning a PhD for a thesis entitled "Might an expanded concept of spiritual memory be the foundation of a new style of Benedictine community dedicated to a dialogue of spirituality with Islam," in 2012. A book based on that thesis was published in September 2013 by Liturgical Press titled *No Peace without Prayer: Encouraging Christians and Muslims to Pray Together; A Benedictine Perspective*. He is now teaching at Benedictine University, Lisle, IL, USA, where some 25 percent of the student body are Muslim.

Mohammad Ali Shomali is a graduate of the Islamic Seminaries of Qum and has both a BA and an MA in Western philosophy from the University of Tehran. He has earned his PhD from the University of Manchester. His publications include *Self-Knowledge* (1996 and 2006, also translated into Malay, Spanish, and Kiswahili), *Ethical Relativism: An Analysis of the Foundations of Morality* (2001, also translated into Malay), *Discovering Shi'a Islam* (7th ed. 2010, also translated into twelve languages), *Shi'a Islam: Origins, Faith and Practices* (2003 and 2010, also translated into Spanish and Swedish), and *Principles of Jurisprudence: An Introduction to Methodology of Fiqh* (2006). He is a coeditor of *Catholics and Shi'a in Dialogue: Studies in Theology and Spirituality* (2004 and 2011), *Catholic-Shi'a Engagement: Reason and Faith in Theory and Practice* (2006 and 2011), and *A Catholic-Shi'a Dialogue: Ethics in Today's Society* (2008 and 2011).

Moshen Javadi is a full professor of philosophy at the University of Qom. He serves as editor-in-chief of the journal *Ethical Research* (published in Farsi by the University of Qom) and the journal *Religious Inquiries* (published in English by the University of Religions and Denominations in Qom). His research focuses on ethics and philosophical theology. Dr. Javadi received his PhD in philosophy from Tarbiat Modarres University in Tehran.

Benoît Standaert is a monk of Sint-Andries Abbey near Bruges (Belgium). He is a biblical scholar and author who teaches at his abbey in the international Institute Gaudium et Spes as well as in Leuven, Milan, and Bangalore. His major work, *L'espace Jésus* (2000), was partially translated into English as *Sharing Sacred Space: Interreligious Dialogue as Spiritual Encounter*, Liturgical

Press, 2009. He brings together exegetical skill, interreligious concern, and a special sensitivity for spirituality.

Farrokh Sekaleshfar completed his medical degree in 2000 at Imperial College London and has been studying at the seminaries in Qum since 2001.

Muhammad Legenhausen (PhD Rice University, 1983) is professor of philosophy at the Imam Khomeini Education and Research Institute in Qum. He is the author of *Islam and Religious Pluralism* (1999) and *Contemporary Topics of Islamic Thought* (2000). Among the works he has translated is *Jesus (peace be with him) through the Qurʾan and Shiʿite Narrations* (2009), collected by Mahdi Muntazir Qaʾim. Among his recent publications is "ʿĀshūrā" (Rome, 2010).

William Skudlarek is secretary general of *Dialogue Interreligieux Monastique* Monastic Interreligious Dialogue. A monk of Saint John's Abbey in Collegeville, Minnesota, and former professor of homiletics and liturgy at Saint John's University, he is now living in Japan as a member of Fujimi Trinity Benedictine Monastery, a dependent priory of Saint John's Abbey.